INDIA'S NONALIGNMENT POLICY

Strengths and Weaknessess

PROBLEMS IN ASIAN CIVILIZATIONS

UNDER THE EDITORIAL DIRECTION OF THE COMMITTEE ON ORIENTAL
STUDIES, COLUMBIA UNIVERSITY

EDITORIAL COMMITTEE: *Wm. Theodore de Bary,* COLUMBIA UNIVERSITY •
Ainslie T. Embree, COLUMBIA UNIVERSITY • *John Meskill,* BARNARD COLLEGE
• *Johanna M. Menzel,* VASSAR COLLEGE • *Arthur Tiedemann,* THE CITY
COLLEGE OF NEW YORK

WANG AN-SHIH — PRACTICAL REFORMER? *Edited by John Meskill*

THE CHINESE CIVIL SERVICE — CAREER OPEN TO TALENT? *Edited by Johanna
M. Menzel*

CHRISTIAN MISSIONS IN CHINA — EVANGELISTS OF WHAT? *Edited by Jessie G.
Lutz*

THE KUOMINTANG DEBACLE OF 1949 — CONQUEST OR COLLAPSE? *Edited by
Pichon P. Y. Loh*

THE PATTERN OF CHINESE HISTORY — CYCLES, DEVELOPMENT, OR STAGNATION?
Edited by John Meskill

1857 IN INDIA — MUTINY OR WAR OF INDEPENDENCE? *Edited by Ainslie T.
Embree*

GANDHI — MAKER OF MODERN INDIA? *Edited by Martin Deming Lewis*

THE PARTITION OF INDIA — CAUSES AND RESPONSIBILITIES. *Edited by T. Walter
Wallbank*

INDIA'S NONALIGNMENT POLICY — STRENGTHS AND WEAKNESSES. *Edited by
Paul F. Power*

DEMOCRACY IN PREWAR JAPAN — GROUNDWORK OR FAÇADE? *Edited by George
O. Totten*

JAPAN 1931–1945 — MILITARISM, FASCISM, JAPANISM? *Edited by Ivan Morris*

Other volumes in preparation

PROBLEMS IN ASIAN CIVILIZATIONS

INDIA'S NONALIGNMENT POLICY

Strengths and Weaknesses

EDITED WITH AN INTRODUCTION BY

Paul F. Power

UNIVERSITY OF CINCINNATI

D. C. HEATH AND COMPANY · BOSTON

Table of Contents

IV. TWO SUMMARY STATEMENTS

Introduction

INDIA's foreign policies have revolved around an "independent" strategy. Often called "nonalignment" and, less accurately, "neutralism," this strategy (which may itself be called a policy) has provided a subject for controversy within and beyond the South Asian state. The conflict of opinion stems from varying and often divergent evaluations of what ideals or realities justify nonalignment, the policy's service to national prestige and security, the merits of changes for its rationale, and the means recommended by critics and defenders. Indian diplomacy in the contest between the Western and Soviet blocs, the need to find substantial economic help from abroad, and the impact of the Sino-Indian dispute on the country's defense and honor have generated much of the discussion of nonalignment. These precipitating factors, important as they are, do not, however, fully explain the importance of the controversy. For out of the debate have come assessments and directives for India's role in world affairs, and these evaluations often go beyond the immediate questions which produced them.

Leading into any discussion of Indian nonalignment are considerations of its sources and the history of the free nation's external relations. Before independence in 1947, India had developed a body of ideas and experiences available for subsequent use in shaping its foreign policies. While some of these notions and experiences did not become important for India's foreign policy, others did influence its framework and style. Among the currents transmitted from the distant past was the Machiavellian advice for rulers in Kautilya's *Arthaśāstra,* dating from the fourth century B.C. Few observers believe that this kind of statecraft has influenced free India's external orientation. However, some Indians, for example the diplomat and historian K. M. Panikkar, have said that India should borrow from Kautilya's ideas. More credit is given to the influence of Buddhist, Hindu, and Jain endorsements of nonviolence, the traditions of pluralism in Hindu society and thought, and historical memories of great rulers, especially Ashoka and the Mogul emperor Akbar. Several observers have found that these currents have, to some degree, marked Indian nationalism and India's foreign policies.

Yet the leaders of modern India chiefly responsible for constructing the directives for India's international conduct were indebted at least as much to Western sources as to their own past. From the impact of and the response to British liberalism and other Western influences came the self-awareness, social awakening and the political stirrings of the nineteenth century that eventually produced Indian nationalism. Although traditionalist and anti-Western in some respects, the growing demand for imperial reform and the devolution of power showed its large debt to Western legal and political concepts, especially after the founding of the Indian National Congress in 1885. As the main vehicle for the rising nationalism, the Congress party attracted and advanced many of the leaders who contributed to the foundations of Indian statehood — Dadabhai Naoroji, Gopal K. Gokhale, Bal Gangadhar Tilak, and Mohandas K. Gandhi. Divided on political tactics and economic policy but eventually united on dislike for British gradualism and belief in Hindu-Muslim coexistence, in the 1920s the Congress party demanded full sovereignty. With the demand came a reaction against India's position in world affairs under British imperialism. Thus a generation before his country's freedom, the scholar-patriot, Taraknath Das suggested from exile in the United States that a liberated India should renounce the balance of power and undertake an independent role in world politics.

Out of the specific contest of Indian nationalism with British imperialism there came a general mistrust of the imperial powers and an overestimation of their strength in international relations. The Soviet Union, however, was welcomed as a friend of anti-colonialism or viewed as no threat of freedom movements. A growing pride in the resurgence of Asia was another important element in nationalist thought, which found expression in Congress party greetings to China's Kuomintang. In the 1930's the Congress spoke out against German and Italian fascism. It also endorsed interstate cooperation and looked forward to a world organization cured of the hegemony of the major Western states discovered in the League of Nations. Pervading representative Congress thinking was the belief that the achievement of Indian sovereignty would release creative forces internally to cure religious communalism and economic underdevelopment, and that externally India's ethical approach to life — said to be proven effective in the nonviolent struggle of the Congress party under Gandhi's leadership — would help to correct the ills of the world.

Of the influences shaping Indian nationalist consideration of world problems in the critical two decades before freedom, Jawaharlal Nehru was crucial in formulating and bringing them to bear on the Congress, the Indian people, and the European rulers. While adhering to Gandhian nonviolence, he developed a neo-Marxian internationalism that Gandhi did not share. Travels in Europe during the 1930's and several disappointments in the struggle for independence enhanced his appreciation of Marxist evaluations of world history. With independence Nehru was the logical choice for Prime Minister and Foreign Minister, dual responsibilities he kept for seventeen years until his death in May 1964.

Nehru had a dominant role in creating India's foreign policies and not merely in restating or managing their content. This function rested on his preeminent leadership in India's foreign and domestic affairs, his full use of vast earned and delegated powers, and his great skill in expressing his beliefs about international relations in notions widely valued in his country, for example, the primacy of peace. In his commanding position Nehru overshadowed his cabinet, the diplomatic corps, and the Congress party. Indicative of his extraordinary power over his nation's foreign relations was the confidential manner in which he could treat correspondence with the Peking government on serious frontier disputes until he permitted White Papers to be published in 1959. After the 1962 border defeats inflicted by China, Nehru's grasp was less certain, and demands grew for a recasting of India's foreign policies.

The creation of free India was at the cost of a partitioning of the Indian subcontinent. The process was accompanied by religious upheavals and economic dislocation that started Indo-Pakistani relations on an unpromising basis. The Kashmir crisis compounded the difficulties. In mid-1947 this predominantly Moslem entity had a princely Hindu ruler who preferred independence from both Pakistan and India to accession to one or the other under the terms of the British withdrawal. In November, tribal raids from Pakistan caused the Maharaja, Sir Hari Singh, to ask for Indian military help. The New Delhi government supplied aid only after receiving his formal request for accession to India and promising on its intiative to hold a plebiscite. The Indian Army secured two-thirds of Jammu and Kashmir, despite the introduction of regular Pakistani troops. In addition to reasons of geography and sentiment, the Nehru government wanted to hold the largely Muslim area in a multi-religious Indian state to demonstrate its secular ideal which Islamic Pakistan denies. India did not, however, find conditions suitable for holding a plebiscite, and New Delhi authorities rejected it as meaningless after Pakistanis crossed the Kashmir cease-fire line in 1965. Not directly relevant to a study of Indian nonalignment, the Kashmir question has, nevertheless, complicated India's independent foreign policy.

When India's constitution went into effect on January 26, 1950, and the state adopted a republican form, the principles to guide its foreign relations were declared to the world through the document's Article 51. It enjoins India

to promote international peace and security; maintain just and honorable relations between nations; foster respect for international law and treaty obligations in the dealings of organized people with one another; and encourage settlement of international disputes by arbitration.

These unexceptional ideas did not explain the political dynamics of the country's foreign relations, which produced demands to be independent of the major blocs, to pursue anti-colonialism everywhere, and to advance economic and social development. On nonalignment a few dissenting voices were heard. In the Constituent Assembly, Hirday Nath Kunzru argued that alignment with the West would best serve Indian interests through association with the leading industrial powers. Looking to Nehru, few Indian leaders agreed then or later, and nonalignment became a basic policy. Pressure on the Nehru leadership to maintain this position came from the left. The Communist party of India contended that the Congress government had a capitalist basis and led India away from the social revolution that must follow sovereignty. This view reflected the Russian standpoint until shortly before Stalin's death that the newly liberated states must choose between the socialist and the capitalist camps. From its emergence in 1949 until its coexistence diplomacy began in 1954, Communist China expressed a similar interpretation of the Nehru government and other nonaligned regimes.

The Korean War brought India more fully into the world arena. Although India endorsed the initial United Nations action to defend South Korea, Nehru restricted Indian aid to a medical unit and tried to mediate the conflict. This Korean policy disturbed the United States. India's objections to military and territorial conditions of the Peace Treaty with Japan in 1951 did not improve official relations between New Delhi and Washington. Subsequently public criticisms in the United States rose when India's positions on numerous issues ranging from arms control to Western rights in Berlin overlapped with Communist positions. Outside of academic circles, there was little American appreciation of India's adherence to the Five Principles of Peaceful Coexistence, or *Panch Shila,* found in the 1954 Sino-Indian Treaty on Tibet and in communiqués which India signed with Communist and nonaligned states. Nehru's initial acceptance of the Soviet version of the 1956 Hungarian revolution caused several Western observers to find a double standard at work. For their part, Nehru and his associates took special exception to American military assistance to Pakistan while refusing President Eisenhower's offer of similar aid to India. India also opposed the creation of defense blocs in the Middle East and Southeast Asia which included Pakistan. The Indian belief that collective security provokes conflicts influenced without controlling the Ten Principles of the 1955 Bandung meeting, where Nehru introduced Chou En-lai to Afro-Asian leaders. This conviction persisted in the policies of Nehru's successors, Lal Bahadur Shastri, and Indira Nehru Gandhi. The belief is inconsistent with the outlook of the United States and its allies, although controversies passed their height in the mid-1950's.

During the late Eisenhower period, the United States began to accept nonalignment as a fact of international life. President Eisenhower's popular visit to India in December 1959 helped to reduce Indian doubts about United States objectives, and the Kennedy and early Johnson years brought a more definite official appreciation of Indian efforts to solve economic and social problems through democratic means. Substantial American aid, economic, technical, and Public Law 480 surplus food sales began to flow to India; and from 1962 to the 1965 hostilities with Pakistan when it was discontinued, important military supplies as well. India has found neither the economic nor the military aid contrary to nonalignment.

Despite improved relations, difficulties have appeared in the 1960's. The Kennedy Administration was displeased over Prime

Minister Nehru's failure to protest the Soviet resumption of nuclear testing in 1961. In the middle of the decade, Indian reliance on American food and the participation of American private enterprise in India's critical fertilizer and related industries were turned into domestic issues by self-reliance enthusiasts and left socialists. Different views on the political issues involved in Vietnam and the use of violence to solve them separated the Gandhi and Johnson governments, although in Indian public opinion there was no major concern about the process and outcome of events in Southeast Asia. The American postponement of Prime Minister Shastri's visit to Washington in 1965, interpreted by him as a reaction to his government's objections to American bombings of North Vietnam, offended Indian pride. Indian criticisms of United States military policies were reinforced by Pakistan's use of American weapons in the April 1965 Kutch crisis and during the wider September conflict between the two neighbors. Mrs. Gandhi's visit to the United States the following spring when President Johnson announced emergency food aid for drought-stricken India improved mutual understanding, but a subsequent delay in Washington's approval of a conventional food pact brought unease in India. American interest in India's future was enhanced by the 1967 General Elections and the renewal of the Congress party's mandate to govern under Mrs. Gandhi's leadership despite its significant electoral losses in the Parliament and the states. The United States' decision in April 1967 not to resume military aid to India or Pakistan led New Delhi to protest that because Pakistan had received many times more supplies than India had secured, Rawalpindi would gain from the new policy which permits only the sale of spare parts for previously supplied equipment. However, should they agree on a common China policy and if their relations with Pakistan and Russia do not collide again, India and the United States might develop closer political ties in and beyond Asia.

Within India few controversies about

foreign policy took place before the Tibetan and Sino-Indian frontier crises of 1959 produced a loss of Indian lives, prestige, and territory. Earlier, Prime Minister Nehru had enjoyed the approval of a public opinion characterized by extensive political illiteracy and conformist political and intellectual elites. The 1959 crises altered these conditions, and Indians began to question the usefulness of *Panch Shila* ideals. The forceful absorption of Goa in December 1961 aided the Nehru government's reputation at home, in Afro-Asia, and the Russian bloc, but not in the West or in China. A year later India's China policy collapsed in military reverses on the northeast border. The Nehru government requested and received immediate American and Commonwealth military help. Few Afro-Asian neutralists proved helpful to India. Soviet arms came later. Indian suspicions of Sino-Pakistani collusion were confirmed when in March 1963 Pakistan signed an agreement with People's China on a "common" frontier in Kashmir which India claims in *toto*. Political results included the resignation of Defense Minister V. K. Krishna Menon, Nehru's associate for many years. Even before China's attacks proved limited and Chinese troops withdrew from seized areas under its unilateral cease-fire, important voices had asked for a reappraisal of Indian foreign policy. Prime Minister Nehru began to show doubts about the value of peaceful intentions in world politics, but he focused on Chinese guilt rather than on Indian errors. Criticism came to a head in August 1963 during a debate on the first motion of censure against the Nehru government in the Indian Parliament. M. R. Masani of the anti-collectivist Swatantra party charged that Indian nonalignment had collapsed because of the government's misunderstanding of Communism together with faulty diplomatic and security measures. The aging Prime Minister and his party overcame the test and reaffirmed their philosophy of nonalignment.

During and after the 1962 frontier difficulties, India continued friendly relations with the Soviet Union. These relations withstood the 1964 changes in Indian and Russian leadership, with the new Soviet regime under Kosygin fulfilling prior pledges to supply military and industrial aid to the Indian government headed by Shastri after Nehru's death in the spring. The Shastri ministry showed its gratitude by efforts to secure Russia's participation as an Asian state in the indefinitely postponed, second Asian-African conference which was to have met in Algiers in the fall of 1965. On his visit to Moscow in May 1965, Prime Minister Shastri pointedly thanked Russia for its respect for Indian nonalignment. The only supplier to continue military aid to India during the Indo-Pakistani hostilities of 1965, Russia secured further political benefits as the peace-maker who brought the two states to sign the Tashkent agreement in January 1966 when Shastri died, making their earlier cease-fire meaningful through troop withdrawals. Although there are many unknowns about the future of Indian and Russian leadership, the Sino-Soviet dispute, and American-Russian relations; because of Nehru's bequest and India's uncertain relations with China and Pakistan, India is likely to continue its favorable interpretations of Russian power in Asian and world affairs.

In response to India's working relations with Russia and the West, People's China has accused India of double alignment. Although the Chinese charge is part of an on-going effort to discredit India, from a military standpoint India's position in world politics makes it eligible for two nuclear shields, a protection for which few states are qualified. If India should want a nuclear defense, it does not have to look to others. For India has its own impressive nuclear program for peaceful purposes which has grown in importance since China exploded its first atomic device in the autumn of 1964 and later moved forward to acquire related capabilities. Some Indian individuals and groups have called for the national development of nuclear weapons, among them the rightist Jan Sangh party. The governing Congress party, however, has periodically reaffirmed its intent to keep India's nuclear technology within peaceful channels even as the Indian program moves toward the production of plutonium without foreign participation and inspection. Reasons for continuing a self-denying policy include past Indian efforts for nuclear pacifism, Western and Soviet advice to remain non-nuclear, the likely disturbance of neighbors by an Indian shift to nuclear weapons, and India's use of its potentiality to encourage nuclear states to reduce their power. The last of these was especially noticeable in 1966 and early 1967 as Russia and the Anglo American states moved closer to an anti-proliferation treaty. If India becomes a nuclear power, Indian nonalignment will be radically altered. The new status for India would make a similar change less difficult for nuclear-ripe countries; India would have taken the main responsibility for disregarding anti-proliferation opinion. Unless the outcome of current instability in China menaces Indian territorial security, India's development of nuclear arms appears unlikely in view of its prevailing values and its economic weakness, anti-proliferation factors which do not depend on the continuation of Congress party rule.

In the perspective of the foregoing sketch of India's foreign relations since freedom, the independent policy of the state may be seen as a major, if not always a unifying, point of reference.

Nearly all segments of Indian political opinion — except the Swantatra party which favors alignment with the West and gained in the February 1967 General Elections — support a continuation of nonalignment. Yet the policy was and is subject to the unsettling effect of contrary forces, such as the challenge of China and domestic and foreign criticism. In response there have been defenses and restatements of the policy. The selections in this book reveal several criticisms and counter-arguments on nonalignment. The concrete questions and answers lead to other questions of this sort: From what values or interests does nonalignment originate? If there is agreement about them, what are the lessons of experience as to fulfilling the norms and interests of nonalignment? Are there newer ideals and stakes that must be served in changed circumstances? For the older or the newer ideals and concerns, what means of implementation are best?

Selections in Part One of this volume reveal various explanations of the origins of India's independent foreign policy. Among the important sources cited are traditional Hindu philosophy, the country's nationalist history, and the realities of underdeveloped and world politics. Within these areas some specific forces said to point to nonalignment are located in Gandhi's ethics, the international thought of Nehru, India's post-freedom opposition to European imperialism, and the search for material aid from affluent states. Opinions differ as to how much weight should be given to a broad source or a formulation within it. Themes introduced in these selections often reappear in more obvious controversies about the values and performance of nonalignment.

Critics of nonalignment appear in Part Two. The need for placing India's foreign policy on a more "realistic" foundation is a general theme of many criticisms, suggesting that a basic task for its study is to relate understandings of declared norms and interests to various objections. Some criticisms focus on the practice of Indian foreign policy, while others examine its premises. Controversy arises from assessments of Nehru's pursuit of freedom for all peoples and his grasp of the nature of interstate relations. In this and other selections of the book, interpretations of Nehru's influence on his country's external affairs during and after his lifetime have a central place without monopolizing the discussion. Critics of Indian nonalignment may notice redeeming features; but in view of new leadership and altered world conditions, they may suggest changes in its means or rationale.

A cross-section of defenses and restatements of nonalignment are grouped in Part Three. They suggest that its theory or practice is either justified or can be reformed to make it sound and effective. Explicitly or implicitly, the writings draw on particular judgments of the values and goals of nonalignment. The tests of India's independent policy by the forceful acquisition of Portuguese India in 1961 and the Sino-Indian hostilities of 1962 receive attention from one or more of the selections. Although Indian relations with Pakistan are not considered at length in this or other selections of this book, the ways in which those relations impinge on Indian nonalignment appear in some readings.

The final section, Part Four, offers two summaries of Indian foreign policy. In the first, a theory of the balancing of power for the welfare of India and the world is the framework for its evaluation of the meaning and prospects of nonalignment. The second uses an "Indian mind" standpoint to begin a review of the diplomatic record and the main issues of India in interstate affairs. The first depends on a relatively fixed theory which is applied to policies and their justifications. Accordingly, nonalignment will have to answer to this theory or else be discarded. The other approach is more organic, viewing nonalignment as a natural product of Indian values and experience. It finds that, like other institutions in the Indian setting, nonalignment will evolve with the times yet continue certain norms and goals. Both readings tend to accept the continuation of nonalignment. They also reflect the influence of criticisms and restatements of nonalignment. The ideas in these and the other selections indicate that the debate about Indian nonalignment continues as an unfinished matter for the largest country under a democratic charter and for those governments and peoples concerned about its future.

[NOTE: *Footnotes have generally been omitted from the selections, except where needed to explain the text.*]

The Conflict of Opinion

"In view of the basic metaphysics of India and the ethics that springs therefrom, it ought not to be difficult to understand India's policy of nonalignment. Although self-realization came only to a few at a given time, the Indian nation as a whole cannot remain at any time uninfluenced by the spiritual culture of this ancient land. We may not be able to trace all the lines that connect our present with the past. Yet, we cannot doubt that there is a connection — and a vital one."

— T. M. P. MAHADEVAN

". . . India's foreign policy has been the product of the interaction of many and varied factors — the traditional values of Indian society, the commitments of the Indian national movement during the struggle for freedom, the nature and structure of elite opinion in India, the geopolitical realities of the state as it emerged from partition, the economic needs of a society urgently in need of a take-off, and the internal political pressures and pulls generated by a democratic system. Subject to the influences exerted by these factors, the foreign policy has sought primarily to pursue India's national interests as conceived by the governing elite."

— SISIR GUPTA

"Speaking in the House in 1958 on *Panchsheel,* I said that it 'was born in sin in as much as by it we put the seal of our approval on the annihilation of a free nation.' Our recognition of Chinese suzerainty over Tibet is in clear contradiction to what our Prime Minister has often said: 'Where freedom is menaced or justice threatened, or where aggression takes place, we cannot and shall not be neutral.' This is dynamic neutrality. In the case of Tibet we have not been even neutral. We have dynamically sided with the aggressor."

— ACHARYA J. B. KRIPALANI

"By applying principles and methods which were premature in the international society, India has not rendered any service to that improvement of the international society which she rightly points to as the great need of mankind. . . . Neutralism then turns out to be not a major contribution to a more peaceful world or even only a peaceful India, but a tool of statecraft that is risky and was mishandled."

— WERNER LEVI

"Both before and after the Sino-Indian encounter, Nehru's government was determined to remain *militarily* non-aligned, in the sense that it was unwilling to enter a Western-sponsored alliance system. Similarly, Indian officials reinterpreted their determination to remain *diplomatically* non-aligned. . . . Ideologically, India's non-alignment was another matter. In whatever degree Indian or American opinion alike often seemed oblivious to the fact, Nehru's government has always been committed to the West ideologically, in the defense of freedom and democratic institutions."

— CECIL V. CRABB, JR.

". . . our nonalignment is understood and welcomed by members of one of the power blocs. The countries of the West have begun to understand it, shifting from their earlier attitudes of ridicule and hostility. They have . . . found it of value in problems where cooperation between the two bloc countries has been essential and in the lowering of international tensions. . . . Nonalignment has thus provided an area (not geographical) of peace in a world where the two blocs are poised against each other."

— V. K. Krishna Menon

". . . the most precious element in the concept of nonalignment has been the instinctive affirmation of India's will to be genuinely independent and a source of influence in her own right. If this is the role that India wills to play, it is inevitable that she must strive to possess sufficient defensive military power, including limited nuclear capability, so that her image is not blurred by her vulnerability. It may sound strange to some, but it is true that limited nuclear armament has now become an inescapable requirement for the preservation of our real independence which constitutes the core of our nonalignment."

— Raj Krishna

"India herself is psychologically unprepared for the manufacture of nuclear weapons. The old foreign policy of India basically remains intact, and, though subjected to various distorting forces, it shows a strong tendency to continue in the channels foreseen for it by Nehru in 1946. It is most unlikely that India will be the next country to enter the nuclear club; but if and when there is another entrant she will feel obliged, though reluctant, to follow suit. . . .'"

—Arthur Lall

I. SOURCES AND VALUES OF NONALIGNMENT

Indian Philosophy and the Quest for Peace

T. M. P. MAHADEVAN

The independent policy of India, states T. M. P. Mahadevan, is based directly on leading ideas of Indian philosophical traditions. The author of this first selection, who is Professor of Philosophy at the University of Madras, discusses the meanings of nonalignment and then examines its sources, which he discovers in the metaphysics of the ancient Upanishads and the ethical teachings of Mohandas K. Gandhi. Professor Mahadevan's analysis is representative of those interpretations which stress the ties between India's philosophical achievements and its contemporary role in world affairs.

In his very first speech as Prime Minister of the Republic of India, Sri Jawaharlal Nehru said, replying to the debate on the President's Address to the Houses of Parliament: "A country's foreign policy ultimately emerges from its own traditions, from its own urges, from its own objectives and more particularly from its recent past." In order to understand the foreign policy of India, one must inquire into India's traditions, urges, and objectives, as well as into its recent past. This is what I propose to do in this paper. But before undertaking the task of such an inquiry, let me state what India's foreign policy is.

The policy of Independent India towards the rest of the world has been described as a policy of neutrality or non-alignment. The word "neutrality," however, is not adequate to express that policy. The Prime Minister said in the speech I have already quoted from: "I dislike the word neutrality, because there is a certain passivity about it and our policy is not passive." On a later occasion he observed,

——I have . . . ventured to point out that whatever policy we were pursuing was not just merely neutral or passive or negative, but that it was a policy which flowed from our past history, from our recent past and from our National Movement and from the various ideals that we have proclaimed from any point of view, whether long-term or short-term that you may apply to the circumstances existing today.

The other word "non-alignment" is probably not so misleading. But whatever term is used, it must be made clear that India's foreign policy is neither passive nor negative. Situated as the world is today, no country can thrive on passivity and negation. And, in spite of what critics of India may hold, the genius of Indian culture is not passive, nor negative.

It has been rightly said that a country's foreign policy is but a projection of its home policy. In a dictatorship, for instance, the dictator wants to make his position secure by compelling his subjects abjectly to surrender to him. For this purpose he creates

From T. M. P. Mahadevan, "India's Policy of Nonalignment," *The Indian Year Book of International Affairs: 1953*, pp. 89–90, 92, 96–105, selections. Reprinted by permission.

one crisis after another, both at home and abroad, and gets his country involved in foreign adventures. India achieved her independence on August 15, 1947, after a long non-violent struggle; and she has resolved to follow the democratic way and adopt a republican form of government. Any newly liberated country will have to face and solve successfully intricate and difficult problems at home. In the case of India, these problems became formidable and assumed huge proportions because of the partition and its black trail of man's inhumanity to man. Under these circumstances, it was wise and natural on the part of the new government of India to have decided not to get their country unnecessarily involved in power politics. Almost from scratch a nation had to be built. From the framing of a constitution and the drafting of a five-year plan to the minutest details of rehabilitating displaced persons, relieving distress caused by famine, floods, etc., the government had to tackle innumerable problems in a constructive and expeditious manner. "The first thing we kept in view," said Sri Nehru in one of his parliamentary speeches,

was to build our own country on solid foundations and not to get entangled in matters which did not directly affect us — not that we are not interested in those matters, but the burden of these entanglements would be too great and the problems we had to face in our own country were big enough for any country to face. . . .

A short-sighted country with an eye on its own immediate advantage may want to exploit the already inflammable situation and align itself with one side or the other. Or, believing in the diplomacy of power politics, and being impelled by considerations of its own interests, a nation may join one or the other of the blocs. India does not fall into either of these categories. It is not her way to adopt a policy that is merely expedient. And she is convinced that a reversion to power politics will only lead to another global war which will surpass all

the previous wars in ghastliness and horror. Speaking about the bleak prospect of a Third World War fought with atomic weapons, Sri Nehru described the atom bomb as a symbol of the incarnate evil and said: "If the force of circumstances compels us, compels the world to use it, it means that the world has surrendered to evil completely." So, it becomes "the duty of everyone to try his utmost to prevent the horror of a Third World War from descending upon us."

The key to India's foreign policy, then, lies in her desire to do all she can to prevent a world catastrophe. In one of his addresses to Parliament, President Rajendra Prasad observed: "While aggression has to be met and evil cannot be condoned, it has to be remembered that war itself is an evil which brings greater evils in its train." To prevent war from overtaking humanity and to promote the cause of world peace — this is the aim of India's foreign policy. "It is the firm policy of my Government," said Dr. Prasad in his very first message to Parliament,

to maintain peace and friendship with all the nations of the world and to help in every way possible in the maintenance of world peace. The Republic of India inherits no enmities or traditional rivalries with other nations and my Government intends continuing a policy directed towards securing peace in the world and avoiding any alignment which leads to hostilities with any nation.

. . . The Great Powers were at first suspicious of India's foreign policy. But now there is increasing appreciation of India's "simple and straightforward" policy and many countries are coming to recognize "the honesty and integrity" of this policy. In his address [October 17, 1949] to Columbia University of the City of New York, our Prime Minister gave expression in a single sentence to the essence of India's foreign policy. He said,

The main objectives of that policy are: the pursuit of peace, not through alignment with any major power or group of powers, but through an independent approach to each controversial or disputed issue; the liberation of subject peoples; the maintenance of freedom, both national and individual; the elimination of racial discrimination; and the elimination of want, disease and ignorance which afflict the greater part of the world's population.

Having explained, in outline, the salient features of India's foreign policy, let me proceed to show that that policy has its foundations in India's culture and traditions, in her religio-philosophic ideology, in her immediate and remote past. This does not, however, mean that India favours a conservative outlook or that she wants to go back instead of moving forward. "In whichever direction we may grow we have to grow out of the roots from which our nation finds sustenance," observed Sri Nehru in one of his Parliamentary speeches, and added,

It is true also that one cannot remain in the roots all the time but one has to grow branches, green leaves and beautiful flowers and therefore one has to adapt oneself and learn from other countries a great deal.

In order to understand the significance of India's foreign policy, one must turn first to her immediate past — the period of struggle for freedom under the leadership of Mahatma Gandhi. He gave to India, and through India to the world, a new conception of politics. The essence of that conception is that the end cannot justify the means, and that everything must be fair in politics. He organized the national fight for independence on the basis of non-violence, and by the success that crowned his efforts, he showed to the world that political objectives can be, and should be, achieved through spiritual means. It was no narrow nationalism that moved Gandhiji[1] to action. He was convinced that if India won her freedom through non-violent means, it would be the largest contribution that any single nation would have made towards world peace. "I do believe," wrote Gandhiji in *Young India* on August 11, 1927,

[1] A term of affection. [Editor's note.]

that if India has patience enough to go through the fire of suffering and to resist any unlawful encroachment upon its own civilization which, imperfect though it undoubtedly is, has hitherto stood the ravages of time, she can make a lasting contribution to the peace and solid progress of the world.

He wished "to see India free and strong so that she may offer herself as a willing and pure sacrifice for the betterment of the world." This, he was convinced, was possible only if India followed the way of non-violence. "If we are to be saved and are to make a substantial contribution to the world's progress, ours must emphatically and predominantly be the way of peace." And, Gandhiji knew perfectly well that India was a fit instrument for delivering the message of non-violence to the world because from time immemorial she has had an unbroken tradition of non-violence.

If India and the world were to be totally non-violent, there should be universal disarmament and government should wither away. Gandhiji was aware that mankind was not ready for the practice of complete non-violence, and that on the attainment of independence by India her armed forces would not be disbanded. So he was advocating only a limited form of non-violence — "non-violence restricted to the purpose of winning our freedom and therefore perhaps for preaching the regulation of international relations by non-violent means."

The example of India, thought Gandhiji, would lead to a better world; and the lessons learnt by India in her non-violent struggle with Britain would be useful in the resolution of international conflicts. The Mahatma was looking forward to the day when India would live on the friendliest of terms with all the nations of the world, be they big or small, and when she would render her good offices in making the nations live in peace. His notion of complete independence for India was not "isolated independence but healthy and dignified interdependence."

The ideal set by Gandhiji for our country is a very lofty one, even with the limitations of which he himself was conscious. It is but natural, therefore, that in our attempt to follow in the footsteps of the Mahatma we should fail sometimes, and fail grievously. Yet, there is no denying the fact that Gandhian ideology is a powerful force influencing our outlook and policy. The Father of the Nation taught us to avoid looking at national and world problems through blood-shot eyes, and exhorted us to "keep our eyes clear." "If I have gained any experience in the last thirty or forty years of my public life," said Sri Nehru in a speech in Parliament on February 3, 1950, "it is this, and certainly if I learnt my lesson from the Great Master who taught us many things it is this that a crooked policy does not pay in the end." Long before he became Prime Minister of India and assumed charge of foreign affairs, Sri Jawaharlal Nehru was specializing in the framing of a policy based on Gandhian principles; for, year after year, at the sessions of the Indian National Congress it was to him that the task of drafting the foreign policy resolution was assigned. And, what he is doing now is to translate that policy into actual practice. India, under his guidance and with the legacy given her by Gandhiji, is pursuing a course in international politics unprecedented in the history of the world — a course which may be described as ethical and spiritual.

No discussion of Indian politics would, probably, be complete, if no reference were made to Kautilya's *Arthaśāstra*.[2] A question that would readily be asked is this: is not the Gandhian ideology fundamentally opposed to the Kautilyan conception of politics? It is presumed that no moral considerations weighed with the Chancellor of Chandragupta Maurya in his policies and actions concerning the affairs of state. It is also taken for granted that there is no alternative Indian or Hindu point of view in politics to that of Chanakya Kautilya.

It is interesting to note, in this connection, that even such a sympathetic student of Indian lore as Heinrich Zimmer goes wrong in his understanding of the political philosophy of India.[3] Drawing his material mainly from Kautilya, he paints a horrid picture of the Hindu conception of politics which he calls "the philosophy of success." What he finds in the *Arthaśāstra* is an advocacy of "the rule of the fish" in politics. "When we review the theories and devices of the Hindu master statesman," says Zimmer,

we behold the ancient style of despotism in all its power and weakness, and begin to understand something of the sinister backgrounds of the Indian political scene: the ever-recurrent tragedy, the constant perils of the individual, the total lack of security, and the absence of all those rights which we cherish today as pertaining to our basic human freedom. In such an atmosphere of threat, dread, and sudden moves, *mātsya-nyāna* prevails, "the law of the fish": the law of life unmitigated by moral decency, as it prevails in the merciless deep.

The king, then, has to be ruthless in his actions against his enemies, and liquidate them by all means possible. Rulership is not for the tender-hearted or the weak-kneed prince. The would-be conqueror (*vijigīṣu*) should be an expert in the art of playing the game of political chess. He should so arrange his moves that no power or combination of powers would be able to defeat him. The kind of political geometry which will enable the king to maintain and augment his position is known as the *maṇḍala*, which is the formula for the arrangement of foreign alliances and coalitions based on "a pattern of concentric rings of natural enemies and allies." By playing off one force against another, by a judicious adjustment of weights and counter-weights, the aspirant for universal empire should achieve his end. There is no question of moral decency here. That policy is good which pays. In inter-statal politics it is "the

---

[2] Essays on the maintenance of political power attributed to an adviser to King Chandragupta Maurya who lived about 322–298 B.C. [Editor's note.]

[3] The reference is to a leading Sanskrit scholar and his book, *Philosophies of India*, ed. by Joseph Campbell (New York, 1951). [Editor's note.]

primeval law of nature" that remains in operation, uncontrolled. It is, in short, the law of the jungle, if "law" it may be called. Zimmer speaks, with disgust, of "the blank pessimism of the Indian philosophy of politics, untouched as it is by any hope or ideal of progress and improvement," and traces to this source

the basic tendency of escape from secular life which characterizes the tradition of classic Indian thought — the holy way of *mokṣa* — the serious search for release from the perils and pains of earthly bondage, through the attainment of some kind of metaphysical equanimity.

And, finally, referring to the contemporary world-situation he makes the unkindest cut of all in the following words:

What is going on today in a large portion of the world would seem, in the light of this book [i.e. *Arthaśāstra*], to amount to a total Asiatization of political affairs, both international and domestic. And the laws are seen again to be what they were in ages past.

Let me point out, even at the outset, that the kind of political strategy that Kautilya recommends to the prince is not something which is peculiar to India or Asia. Right from the dawn of history in Europe one finds there an almost continuous struggle for dominance by one power over another. With the rise of Christendom, even the church entered the arena of political strife. And when, with the opening of the modern era, church hegemony was put an end to, the various nation-states became rivals in their earth-hunger and power-madness. The history of the last three hundred years is one of Western powers exploiting Oriental peoples and prospering at the latters' expense. When the eyes of nations become blind with a passion for political domination, no value is attached to the sameness of race, religion or tradition. The struggle for colonies was mainly between European nations. And in the two world wars the chief belligerents were Western nations. So, the West need not

come to Asia for a training in *mātsya-nyāya*. Zimmer himself recognizes this when he says, "This is a law no less well known to the West than to India."

As regards Kautilya, in order to arrive at a fair judgement, one must take into account the age in which he lived and the part he had to play in the political revolution of his time. The fourth century B.C. was an unsettled age in India. Alexander had invaded the country. The Nandas had become unpopular, corrupt and weak. It was at that time that Chandragupta Maurya rose to power with the assistance of Kautilya. And, the Mauryan revolution was justified in the sense that the whole of North India became unified, and the Indus Valley was emancipated from foreign yoke.

It is against this background that we must attempt an estimate of Kautilya. His *Arthaśāstra* is not a treatise on political philosophy. It is a guidebook on statecraft. Kautilya, certainly, does not prescribe the law of the fish for the affairs of a state. On the contrary, he insists that the rule of law must prevail in the state. Even the sovereign must submit to law. Says Kautilya, "Whatever sovereign, even one whose domination extends to the ends of the earth, if of perverted disposition and ungovernable senses, must quickly perish." Dharma or the rule of law supplants the law of the jungle. A state cannot function in the absence of mutual goodwill, forbearance, and co-operation among individuals and groups.

Even Zimmer acknowledges that this is the Indian — and Kautilyan — view. Only he would still say that "this peaceful pattern of well-controlled, harmonious human decency" can never be transferred, according to the Indian conception, to the larger field of the nations. Here too it would be an advantage to understand the context in which the *Arthaśāstra* was written. Kautilya was not confronted with the problem of international relations, as we use the term today. All that he was concerned with was the unification of the country under a central authority. He does not profess to lay down a code of conduct for the nations.

But this much is true, that for the purpose of achieving the end of political unity, he was prepared for the adoption of any means, whether right or wrong, moral or immoral. This, however, ought not to be taken as the typical Hindu view. Later writers like Bāṇa have criticized Kautilya. It is not the teaching of the Indian philosophy of politics that even as between states the rule of the beasts should prevail. *Artha* or polity should be rooted in *dharma* or righteousness. That kings and statesmen in India, as elsewhere, relied often on the expedient rather than on the good might be a fact. But that does not mean that the wise men of India commended or condoned unethical ways of achieving and safeguarding political power. The ideal of *Rāma-rājya* as depicted in the epic, *Rāmāyaṇa*, and the conduct of Emperor Aśoka, after the Kalinga war are some of the glowing examples to which one should turn for understanding the spirit of the Indian philosophy of politics. To characterize the Indian conception of politics as pessimism is, therefore, unjust. And, to say that the gloomy view of life in the secular state is responsible for the doctrine of *sannyāsa* (which Zimmer calls escape) is to convey no meaning at all. *Sannyāsa* does not stand for defeatism or a sense of frustration. The *sannyāsin* is not the one who runs away from the world or from life. On the contrary, it was his counsel that used to be sought even in matters concerning the state. And, when we come to the Gandhian ideology, we have a thorough integration of the spirit of *sannyāsa* with every aspect of political life.

Probably, many may not object to an attempt to show that our foreign policy stems from the teachings of Gandhiji. But many may not know that that policy reflects — however imperfectly — the philosophic culture and religious tradition of India.

The most lofty heights of metaphysical realization were reached by the seers of the Upanishads which have been aptly described as the Himalayas of the soul. Here we come across a view of Reality which has no parallel in any other thought-system of the world.

Brahman or *Ātman* which are the expressions used in the Upanishads for the ultimate Reality is unconditioned, undifferentiated, non-dual spirit. It is a *nirguṇa*, qualityless, in the sense that it cannot be defined in terms of any of the known attributes. To qualify it, to predicate any characteristic of it, is to negate its non-duality. To indicate its nature, without involving it in limitations, the Upanishads adopt the *via negativa* and say "It is not this, not this" (*neti neti*). This, however, does not mean that Brahman is a contentless vacuity. The Supreme Reality is the plenitude of being (*sat*), pure consciousness (*cit*), and unconditionad bliss (*ānanda*). Such terms should not be understood in their ordinary sense. They represent the highest concepts the mind of man has succeeded in evolving to indicate the nature of the supreme Spirit. Words and ideas are but poor vehicles to make us understand the highest truth. One understands by being it, and not through the ordinary channels of knowledge. That was why an Upanishadic sage, as reported by Shankara, remained quiet when asked to explain the nature of the Self (*śānto'yam ātmā*). Peace is the name by which the Self is to be known. It is perfect peace because there is no "other" to it. It is non-dual (*advaita*). Consciously or unconsciously, India has been influenced by this ideal of a reality where there is no room for struggle or strife — a reality that is not divided, that is not-two (*advitīya*). Mahatma Gandhi once wrote, "I believe in *advaita*, I believe in the essential unity of man and, for that matter, of all that lives." Sri Jawaharlal Nehru, in his *Discovery of India* has expressed his predilection for *advaita*. One of the members of Parliament gave expression to his hope that the principle of our foreign policy is "the neutrality of the spirit which we would like the world as a whole to adopt."

The ideal of Indian spirituality is sagehood which is the state of equanimity and sameness of attitude towards all beings. An oft-quoted verse of the Bhagavadgita reads thus: "The wise ones look with the same eye on a *brāhmaṇa* possessed of learning and humility, a cow, an elephant, a dog, and even a dog-eater" (v. 18). The concluding stanzas (56ff) of chapter two of the Gita, the recitation of which used to form an invariable feature of Gandhiji's prayer-meetings, give a description of the sage whose wisdom is secure (*sthita-prajña*). The wise one who has attained to perfect knowledge has an equal-vision which is unperturbed when confronted with the opposites of pleasure and pain, praise and blame, etc., which are the inevitable constituents of life. He has risen above the passions that storm and distract the soul, and is firmly established in the "peace that passeth understanding." His inner placidity never gets disturbed, for he has no wants or desires. In him all enjoyments find their consummation, even as in the ocean all the waterways merge themselves. The moral of the whole description is that the sage is not swayed by attachments and hatred. Similarly, the Lord of the Gita says about himself that he is the same to all beings, and that there is none hateful or dear to him (ix, 29).

The concept of sameness (*samatva*), however, does not mean that either the sage or God is indifferent to the good of the world. The perfect being is ever solicitous of the welfare of all beings. The sage loves all and elevates all. Writing about the Vedantic ideal, Deussen[4] observes that to the question "Why should I love my neighbour as myself" the answer of the Upani-shads is: Because your neighbour is yourself.

Or, in the words of the Bhagavadgita: he who knows himself in everything and everything in himself, will not injure himself by himself, *nahinasti ātmanā ātmānam*. This is the sum and tenor of all morality, and this is the standpoint of a man knowing himself as Brahman.

That humanity is one family — nay, that all living beings constitute one kindred group is a fundamental teaching of Hinduism. This is the reason why such great emphasis is laid on the practice of *ahiṁsā*. Though this term has a negative form "non-violence," it has a positive implication which is "active love towards all beings." It is this glorious ideal of universal love and total peace that is expressed in the Hindu prayer:

sarvas taratu durgāṇi, sarvo bhadrāṇi paśyatu, sarvas tad-buddhim āpnotu, sarvas sarvatra nandatu.

"May all beings safely cross the hazards and hardships of life! May all see the beaming face of happiness! May all gain the knowledge of Truth. May there be universal rejoicing!"

In view of the basic metaphysics of India and the ethics that springs therefrom, it ought not to be difficult to understand India's policy of non-alignment. Although self-realization comes only to a few at a given time, the Indian nation as a whole cannot remain at any time uninfluenced by the spiritual culture of this ancient land. We may not be able to trace all the lines that connect our present with the past. Yet, we cannot doubt that there is a connection — and that a vital one.

---

[4] Paul Jacob Deussen, author of *Outlines of Indian Philosophy: The Philosophy of the Vedanta* to which reference is made. [Editor's note.]

National Interest and World Reform

SISIR GUPTA

In contrast to the first selection's emphasis on one major origin of Indian nonalignment, this reading suggests that several formative influences were involved. Sisir Gupta is Research Secretary of the Indian Council of World Affairs and the author of studies dealing with Kashmir and other problems in Indo-Pakistani relations. His analysis also differs from the Mahadevan essay in finding that national interest has been the major guide for India's foreign policy. Yet Sisir Gupta also believes that India has values to offset its material weakness and to make it a reforming power in international politics.

Interpreting his country's foreign affairs after a decade and a half of experience, he pays special attention to India's relations with the great blocs and to a comprehensive view of the Sino-Indian controversy. As do other Indian scholars and publicists who adhere to a national interest perspective, Sisir Gupta offers reasons to explain and justify nonalignment which are at least as didactic as they are practical.

INDIA's foreign policy has been the product of the interaction of many and varied factors — the traditional values of Indian society, the commitments of the Indian national movement during the struggle for freedom, the nature and structure of elite opinion in India, the geopolitical realities of the State as it emerged after partition, the economic needs of a society urgently in need of a take-off, and the internal political pressures and pulls generated by a democratic system. Subject to the influences exerted by these factors, the foreign policy has sought primarily to pursue India's national interests as conceived by the governing elite. It is in terms of this primary motivation that the enunciation and evolution of India's foreign policy has to be viewed.

In one of his early speeches in the Indian Parliament, the Prime Minister stated:

Whatever policy you may lay down, the art of conducting the foreign affairs of a country lies in finding out what is most advantageous to the country. We may talk about international goodwill and mean what we say. We may talk about peace and mean what we say. But in the ultimate analysis, a government functions for the good of the country it governs and no government dare do anything which in the short or long run is manifestly to the disadvantage of the country . . . whether a country is imperialistic or Socialist or Communist, its Foreign Minister thinks primarily of that country. . . .

It was not possible for the new Government of India, however, to define India's national interests in the way of the outgoing Raj. On the contrary, they were bound by their past commitments as well as the present realities to totally reevaluate these concepts. In the first place, the succeeding Government of India was not as powerful as the previous one. Secondly, India's partition had considerably reduced the geographical extent of the Indian State. Thirdly, the very upsurge of national sentiments which led to the freedom of India was bound to be felt elsewhere and ex-

From Sisir Gupta, *India and Regional Integration in Asia* (New York, 1964), pp. 1–11, 14–26, selections. Reprinted by permission.

pressed in the form of resentment to any new approach of domination. Fourthly, India's emergence in the world coincided with the emergence of a vast ideological confrontation in the world, which was backed by the changed power realities of the European and American continents. Lastly, much of the old strategic concepts were ruled out by the development of nuclear arms and the emergence of air power as the major weapon of war.

Functioning within these limitations, India had to evolve a foreign policy which would advance not only her own security but, what was immensely more urgent for her, the status of the country in international politics. It was through the advancement of this status that India sought to attract attention and sympathy for her and similarly-placed countries and also to underline the significance of the new countries in the context of global politics. One might indeed say that in the early years of her foreign policy India was pursuing the understandable search for a short cut to international status.

Speaking in the Indian Parliament on 8 March 1948, Nehru said:

. . . our responsibility is very little. We may have acted well or badly on the international stage, but we are not, frankly speaking, influential enough to affect international events very much.

A year later, speaking at a public meeting in New Delhi, the Prime Minister said:

We are as an independent country, a fairly young country at present . . . and therefore our foreign policy is gradually developing and there is no particular reason why we should rush in all over the place and do something that comes in the way of this gradual development.

Speaking in the Parliament on 6 December 1950, Nehru said: "The fate of the world depends more on the USA, the United Kingdom, the Soviet Union and China than on the rest of the world put together."

In a penetrating analysis of the ultimate needs of India's functioning in world affairs the veteran Indian Civil Servant, G. S. Bajpai, then the Secretary General of India's External Affairs Ministry, wrote in 1952:

India then has to develop her strength to support her foreign policy. The inherent goodness of that policy is insufficient to sustain or further it. On this view the inference that politics cannot be divorced from power holds true also for India. . . . Today, India is the major stabilizing factor for peace in Asia; the measure of stability that she can impart to this part of the world is not a matter of good intentions but of power. . . . It is not power but its misuse or abuse which is morally reprehensible. . . . Thus viewed the ideal of balance of power is nothing evil or incompatible with India's highest ideals.

It is consciousness of the inability of India to play any significant role in the traditional sense of diplomacy backed by power that governed much of the foreign policy thinking and behaviour of the country.

It is not, however, the prospects of an inevitable reconciliation with the status of insignificance that the Indian leaders faced. Much as the country was militarily insignificant, it represented an entirely new element in world politics, of which the potential strength was of great importance. Two factors made India strong in her foreign policy functioning: in the first place, as virtually the first and the biggest of the newly-freed countries of Asia and Africa, her voice was bound to count for something in a world where decolonialization was on the agenda; and, secondly, by itself, India represented a vast country with a huge population, the future of which was bound to affect the course of an important section of mankind.

This consciousness of India's strength was particularly apparent to the Indian Prime Minister who had been known for his capacity to view events in the canvas of history. In one of his early speeches, he said:

The fact of the matter is that in spite of our weakness in a military sense . . . India even today counts in world affairs. . . . If we had been some odd little nation somewhere in Europe or Asia it would not have mattered much. But because we count and because we are going to count more and more in the future, every thing we do becomes a matter for comment.

Dwelling on the positional importance of India, Nehru said in another speech: "Now that period and epoch (of European domination) has ended and India now comes, I think, into the forefront in national events and world affairs."

It is the announcement of this arrival of India in the international arena which was evidently the major preoccupation of the Prime Minister in so far as his early speeches are concerned. In carrying out this immediate post-Independence task, the Prime Minister of India stressed two aspects: the crucial role of Asia in world affairs of the impending decades; and, the pivotal position of India in Asia.

Declaring the need for recognizing that a revolution was under way in Asia, Nehru carefully emphasized the nature of this revolution and the difference between the problems of Asia and the relatively more-developed regions of the world. In fact, much of the essence of India's foreign policy outlook is contained in the early speeches of Jawaharlal Nehru proclaiming the emergence of Asia.

Inaugurating the Asian Relations Conference in New Delhi on 23 March 1947, the Prime Minister of India said:

We stand at the end of an era and on the threshold of a new period of history. Standing on the watershed which divides two epochs of human history and endeavour, we can look back on our long past and look forward to the future that is taking shape before our eyes. Asia after a long period of quiescence has suddenly become important again in world affairs.

The theme continued to dominate his speeches throughout the early years of

Indian freedom; he took particular care to stress it before his Western audiences. Speaking at the eleventh session of the Institute of Pacific Relations on 3 October 1950, Nehru said:

While people readily agree that Asia has, to a certain extent, become the focal point of world tension, they relegate the Asian problems to the positions of relative insignificance and tend exclusively to emphasize the importance of European and other world problems. . . . In the perspective of things to come they were wrong in not devoting the requisite attention to the problems of developing Asia.

This complaint was made earlier. "Even in the councils of the United Nations, the problems of Asia, the outlook of Asia, the approach of Asia, have failed to evoke the enthusiasm that they should."

The need to underline the problems that the Asian situation posed was one of the first tasks of Indian foreign policy. The problems of Asia were not the problems of Europe and any attempt at the identification of the two was bound to understate the Asian case in the world. As Nehru put it:

There are many ways of distinguishing between what may be called the approach of Asia and the approach of Europe. Asia today is primarily concerned with what may be called the immediate human problems. In each country of Asia — underdeveloped countries, more or less — the main problem is the problem of food, of clothing, of education, of health. We are concerned with these problems. We are not directly concerned with problems of power politics.

Again: "Asia compels attention in many ways. . . . But what is most needed is an understanding that Asia is going through a process of change and that it is in ferment." The problems of Asia were primarily social and economic, and as the political domination by Europe was ending, long-term problems were being thrown up by the revolutionary ferment. . . .

It is the policy of nonalignment in the

cold war which lent to Indian policy the distinctive characteristics which have at once made it controversial and complex. It is not relevant here to describe the foreign policy in detail or to indicate the specific Indian views on major world problems dividing the great Powers. What needs to be emphasized in connection with the subject-matter under review, however, is that the policy of nonalignment was basically an instrument of pursuing the goals of India's national interests; it is, therefore, not the negative aspect of this policy of remaining aloof from the cold-war alignments but the more positive attempt implicit in this policy of emerging as the area of agreement between the great Powers of the world, which should be considered the core of India's foreign policy.

The national needs of India were well stated by Nehru himself: ". . . in the long run, it is to the advantage of India to try to attract to itself the sympathy and the hope of millions of people in the world without offending others." Nonalignment, as such, was relevant to the extent that any Indian decision to line up in the cold war might tend to freeze that part of the world. India's primary interest was not in arresting the revolution that was inevitably unfolding itself in the area but to so mould it as to be consistent with the needs of world peace and freedom. In this sense, India's foreign policy is inextricably bound up with the internal approach to her problems. The three basic planks of India's State policies — nonalignment in world affairs, a democratic and liberal political system, and an increasing governmental participation in the economic life of the community in order to force the pace of economic growth — are all meant to serve the twin objectives of unleashing the revolution and phasing it, objectives which could become the basis for her friendly posture to both the great Powers of the world.

Most of these objectives were well stated by Nehru himself, although the burden of his office increasingly made him circumspect in his speech. Referring to the initial disadvantages of a policy of nonalignment, he said:

. . . there was suspicion in the mind of one group that we were really allied to other groups . . . and the other group thought we were really allied to the other group in secret though we were trying to hide the fact.

Nehru said in a tone of apparent confidence on 4 December 1947:

Nonetheless, that [nonalignment] is the only honourable and right position for us to take and I am quite sure that by adopting that position, we shall ultimately gain in national and international prestige, that is to say, when we take a long view of the situation, not a short view of immediately getting a vote here or there. . . I have no doubt that fairly soon, in the course of two or three years, the world will find this attitude justified and India will not only be respected by the major protagonists in the struggle for power, but a large number of smaller nations which today are rather helpless will probably look to India more than to other countries for a lead in such matters. . . .

Again:

Our policy will continue to be not only to keep aloof from power alignment, but to try to make friendly cooperation possible. Fortunately, we enter upon our independence as a country with no hostile background in regard to any country. We are friendly to all countries . . . we approach the whole world on a friendly basis and there is no reason why we should put ourselves at a disadvantage, if I may say so, by becoming unfriendly to any group.

Underlying this policy is an assumption which was not shared by many other countries in the world: the nature of the Communist bloc is neither monolithic nor is there any inevitable expansionist tendency of the Communist bloc as a whole. What is more, to the extent that communism poses a social, economic, and political challenge internally in all these countries, it has to be answered in social, economic, and political terms. An undue emphasis on the military challenge might not only detract attention from these spheres of policy but prove self-defeating by eroding the flexibility and vitality of the democracies in Asia. A posture of status quo for any Asian (or African) country would isolate it from the main historical trends in the region and leave communism as the only ideology seeking radical solutions for difficult situations. . . .

From . . . statements made by the Indian Prime Minister, it is clear that in the Indian conception of the Communist problem, the military aspects of the challenge of communism were relatively unimportant; what is important, however, is to establish the superiority of the democratic system, even for Asian and other backward countries. In this sense the rise of Communist China, though posing a problem for India in many fields, was not entirely an evil. Between them, communism and nonalignment performed the very necessary function of underlining the nature of the basic problems faced by Asia in its phase of resurgent revolution. The divergence between the Indian and American outlook in the matter of China emanated from this basic evaluation of the nature of the new [Chinese] State.

It must be added, however, that it would not be entirely correct to say that India did not take into account the military problem that China posed for her security; as early as December 1950, the Indian Government made it clear that it recognized the threat when it unilaterally extended guarantee to the northern neighbour, Nepal. The Himalayas involved India's security and none would be allowed to cross it (into Nepal) without confronting India. Also significant was the initiative that India took in arranging Commonwealth economic and military aid to Burma [in 1949] to stave off the Communist threat. It was a tactic therefore — vital in the context of the overall requirements of India's national interests — to understate this aspect of the problem in order to be able to meet with international support the more challenging task of competing with China in other spheres.

In the internal sphere there was little softness demonstrated in the treatment of the Communists, although they were allowed to function freely after 1951, when they gave up their aim of immediate revolution in India. In fact, the Prime Minister of India has in his speeches and statements maintained a constant offensive against the local Communist party as well as the Communist doctrines as a whole. Speaking shortly after the Bulganin-Khrushchev visit to India [in 1955], Nehru said:

Let us come to the Communists — these brave revolutionaries whose revolution consists not in application of intelligence but in trying to find out what is happening 5000 miles away, and trying to copy it, whether it fits in or not with the present state of India. . . . Unfortunately, our friends of the Communist Party of India have so shut their minds and have so spent all their time and energy in learning a few slogans of the past that they are quite unable to appreciate what is happening in India. In fact, these great revolutionaries of the Communist Party of India have become great reactionaries.

Talking in 1960 to an Indian journalist, Nehru said in a reference to Marxism:

There is no proletariat of the Marxist conception in America . . . although the logical reasoning of Marx was correct, other factors have intervened. The sum of them . . . that is these new factors and particularly the two features I have mentioned of political democracy and technological advance . . . have produced a new set of conditions and Marxism must be reviewed in this new context.

Earlier [in 1958], Nehru had made a cogent criticism of the Marxist philosophical system and the irrelevance of it in the new situation while enunciating his "basic approach" to politics; the publication of this brought a sharp retort from the Communist world, accusing Nehru in classical Marxist terms of practising violence on the proletariat while professing nonviolence, etc. In fact, the publication of these Nehru-

Yudin[1] exchanges made it clear that a section of the Communist world was preparing for a decisive onslaught on the Nehru position in politics. . . .

One of the basic assumptions of India's foreign policy on which much of its validity rests is that the Communist world is not only not monolithic but that hopes must be placed on its ultimate disintegration and the rise of liberal forces inside the Communist world. One of the possible reasons for India's initial enthusiasm for China was the fact that Soviet Communism under Stalin had described India as the lackey of imperialism and attempted to foment revolts within India. The fact that Mao's revolution was self-propelled in nature meant a possible breakthrough in Communist solidarity and rigidity. In spite of the obvious difficulty for any official statement to mention it, Nehru said in the Indian Parliament in December 1950:

China is in a position to shape her own destiny and that is a great thing. It is true that she is controlled by the Communists as Russia is. It would be interesting to know whether or not their type of communism is the same as Russia's, how she will develop, and how close the association between China and Russia will be.

The Indian Press went further than this in explaining this. *The Tribune* wrote that the U.S. position in regard to China "only serves to promote the interest of the Soviet Union," and added:

Few Americans seem yet to grasp the obvious fact that Mr. Nehru's China policy is not designed to strengthen Communist imperialism but to weaken it by demonstrating to the people of China that their friends are to be found not among the Communist States alone but everywhere.

This initial hope in China was replaced by a hope in the prospect of liberalization in the Communist Party of the Soviet

[1] M. Yudin, Russian Ambassador to China in 1958, who responded to Nehru's criticism of Marxism. [Editor's note.]

Union, after the process of destalinization had been started by the Twentieth Congress of the party. Welcoming the change, Nehru made a statement in the Indian Parliament:

I should like to take this opportunity of drawing the attention of the House to a very important event in recent weeks. I refer to the Twentieth Congress of the Communist Party of the Soviet Union which met recently in Moscow. There can be no doubt that this Congress has adopted a new line and a new policy. This new line, both in political thinking and practical policy, appears to be based upon a more realistic appreciation of the present world situation and represents a significant process of adaptation and adjustment. . . . We feel that the decisions of the Twentieth Congress of the Soviet Union are likely to have far-reaching effects. I hope that this development will lead to a further relaxation of tension in the world.

It is during the subsequent years of the growing China-India rivalry and conflicts that this approach was further underlined in Indian policy statements. During his last visit to the United States [in 1961], the Indian Prime Minister was reported to have remarked in his off-the-record conversations that "Mr. Khrushchev sees India as a future bulwark against China and that it is in the Soviet interest to help restrain Peking." Naturally, much of this hope remains unstated publicly; but there have been enough official statements to show the extent to which the USSR is depended upon in the conflict with China.

The basic Indian assumption would seem to be that as the Soviet society is transforming itself from a backward to an advanced economy and the pent-up consumption urge of the Soviet people is seeking satisfaction, there is bound to be an increasing stake felt by the Soviet Union in the peaceful resolution of world problems. . . . Apart from this assumption in regard to the politics in the Communist world, India has emerged as a factor in that politics and it is obviously one of the objectives of its foreign policy to continue to be so. It is the

least publicly talked of aspect of the motivations of Indian policy; for, obviously,
public expression of this can become self-
defeating. But pieces of evidence suggest
that India regards it as of tremendous consequence to be able to remain an item of
controversy inside the Communist bloc.

It may be said with some justification
that in the whole debate in the Communist
world over the nature and role of what has
been officially described in recent Communist documents as the "national democracies,"[2] India has been the focal point of
conflict. The Chinese decision to make a
direct assault on relations with India cannot be separated from the fact that it was
necessary for her struggles within the Communist bloc to prove that the neutral nations like India were not in reality neutral
and posed a long-term problem for the
Communists.

The fact that India has joined issue with
the left-wing Communists in the inner
debate of the Communist world is clearly
illustrated from the following extract from
a speech by Nehru in the Indian Parliament in late 1959:

China is very, very far from normality, and
that is our misfortune and the world's misfortune. . . . That is, strength, considerable
strength, coming in an abnormal state of
mind. . . . That is why you find a marked
difference between the broad approach of the
Soviet Union and the Chinese approach. I
do not think there is any country in the world
which is more anxious for peace than the
Soviet Union. . . . But I doubt if there is any
country in the world . . . which cares less for
peace than China today. . . . The world is
changing and I can conceive of the two great
colossuses today, the Soviet Union and the
United States, coming very near to each
other, as they are slightly coming. . . . This
talk about international capitalism and international communism, reflecting an old slogan,
merely prevents us from thinking straight and
understanding the changed world.

[2] A category of ex-colonial nations identified at
the November 1960 meeting of world Communist
parties in Moscow as "progressive" and capable of
development into the socialist camp. [Editor's
note.]

It is also to be noted here that the nature
of the Soviet and Chinese advice to the
Indian Communist Party has been different; also different has been the official
Indian attitude in the matter of the Communist Party's links with Moscow and
Peking. In the last Congress of the Indian
Communist Party at Vijayawada, held in
April 1961, the Chinese could not attend
the conference but the chief Soviet guest at
the Conference, Suslov, was accorded welcome by officials of the Indian Government.

Just as India has not remained non-
aligned in the internal conflict of the
Communist world, she has found herself
involved in the politics of the Western
bloc. It is now known that both in the
Indo-Chinese and the Korean conflicts,
India was regarded as a friend by the British Government, while she was sometimes
regarded as an unwanted intruder by the
United States. . . .

Even when the crisis in Egypt began [in
1956], India attempted to understate the
British role in fomenting the crisis; but as
the crisis advanced and ultimately resulted
in the invasion, Indo-British relations suffered a setback. It is of interest to note that
it is in this period that, following the
Indian Prime Minister's visit to the United
States in December 1956, the relations between India and the United States began
to improve.

It is this aspect of India's foreign policy
—the attempt to remain a factor in inner-
bloc politics while remaining generally
nonaligned in the cold war—which needs
to be emphasized. For, no policy evolved
for a closer association of nations of the
[Asian] region or the nonaligned in general
which would tend to take the unity of the
rival cold-war blocs and their inclination to
wage this cold war for granted would be
consistent with the needs of India, or with
her conception of the needs of the neutral
or the nonaligned world.

These needs as conceived by India are of
paving the way for greater international
cooperation through the mitigation of cold
war and the underlining of those issues in

world politics which should be able to transcend the cold war. The hopes of backward regions of delivering the goods internally depended largely on their capacity to utilize the growing surplus of the advanced countries generated by a vastly improved technology and the constant technological revolution under way. The need for these countries was not so much to exert the strength that they potentially possessed but to invoke international cooperation in the solution of their vital problems. In this respect India's approach was distinguishable from that of some other countries which would defy both the great Powers and regard them as monsters rather than attempting to devise possible bases for their cooperation, at least in the field of the problems of the underdeveloped world.

This assumption that any mitigation of the cold war and the arms race was bound to throw up areas like India as the problem areas of the world demanding cooperation from all developed regions, irrespective of their ideology, led to the Indian emphasis both on the possibility and desirability of U.S.-U.S.S.R. rapprochement. There was an obvious area of agreement between the two great Powers, according to India, and a common stake in certain spheres of world developments. . . .

The Indian interest in U.S.-U.S.S.R. rapprochement was heightened by the feeling that among the visible areas of agreement between the Power blocs, particularly the great Powers, India was a major item. In his reply to a question whether the big Powers could make India the laboratory of the next phase of Soviet-American economic coexistence on the basis of helping to reconstruct the underdeveloped world, Nehru said in 1960:·

. . . both are cooperating with us in a big way. There is Bhilai[3] and there are American projects, British projects, Canadian projects,

[3] A Russian-built, public iron and steel complex. After the United States declined for reasons of technical feasibility, Russia agreed to help build a second complex at Bokaro which is scheduled for completion in late 1970. [Editor's note.]

German projects in our development plans. . . . The important fact is that there is realization of what you called economic coexistence, although at present it is developing more on a competitive than cooperative basis. But the latter is bound to follow.

Again, towards the end of the conversation, the Prime Minister said:

. . . today there is an almost universal understanding and appreciation of what we are trying to do on the economic plane . . . that is planning under a democratic pattern of socialism. This has set a new pattern for Asian and African development and it is significant that economists and other experts from both the worlds, particularly the West to which economic planning is something foreign, are extremely interested in development plans and progress. . . . This makes India itself a kind of an area of agreement between the opposing ideological forces. Without boasting about it we can claim to be the only underdeveloped country trying to do it in a big way. . . .

It may be pertinent to sum up the Indian view of the world in the following terms: apart from the generally recognized line dividing the world, that between the Communist and the non-Communist world, there is another and a more formidable, albeit subdued, dividing line at work. This is the line dividing the developed and the underdeveloped world. What makes this line more pernicious and explosive in the long run is that it broadly coincides with two other lines dividing the peoples of the world; it so happens that the developed world is in the main the white and the underpopulated part of the world and the under-developed the coloured and the overpopulated. If this line is taken into account, it cuts across the line dividing the Communist and the non-Communist world. From the viewpoint of this division, the Indian and the Chinese pattern of development have different connotations; it is inherent in the nature of Chinese development, based on the mobilization of manpower by whipping up an entire sleeping population and putting them to spartan discipline to build up State power, that where conflicts exist they will be sharpened. It is the dynamic of the Indian approach to development, based on the cooperative utilization of the surplus of the developed regions, that it will stress international cooperation and peaceful resolution of conflicts. To the extent that the Chinese approach is bound ultimately to challenge the structure of world politics, there is a common stake of the great Powers to promote the Indian experiment. Her proximity to China, the size of her population and the inevitable influence that she exerts on other peoples of the region make India somewhat like the developed nations' model farm in the underdeveloped world. The basic objectives of India are to remain in this position and demonstrate the possibility of solving the problems of similarly-placed countries with the cooperation and sympathy of the great Powers of the world.

II. CRITICS OF NONALIGNMENT

Inconsistencies and Failures

ADDA B. BOZEMAN

The American image of India as a philosophical civilization is the point of departure for this critical evaluation of Indian foreign policy. Adda B. Bozeman is Professor of History, Law and International Relations at Sarah Lawrence College and author of *Politics and Culture in International History*. Her appraisal focuses on Nehru's political thought as the main source of the premises on which nonalignment rests. She finds a paradox between the Indian leader's international assumptions and what he expected of his nation's political system. She also discovers a pattern of inconsistencies between India's declared intentions and its actual behavior in the cold war. The question of how well the Nehru government provided for national security is also considered. Overall, this analysis represents those criticisms of nonalignment that judge it faulty because of ideological preference and inattention to territorial security.

OCCIDENTAL nations had distinct images of India long before they recognized the new republic ten years ago. To Herodotus and his contemporaries India was the scene of fabled wonders; to devout Christians in the Middle Ages it was the likely site of Paradise; and to the learned of later enlightened centuries it was above all the abode of superior wisdom. In fact, nothing about India seems to have attracted Western scholars so much as the religions and philosophies that originated in the subcontinent millennia ago. The fundamental principles of Hinduism, Jainism, and Buddhism were analyzed and exposed with scholarly care during the nineteenth and early twentieth centuries, as Western minds, increasingly convinced of the essential "materialism" of their own heritage, made a steady pilgrimage to the repositories of the great spiritual truths that India held. Subjects of a more materialistic nature, on the other hand, such as the actual manifestations of the great religions, the social systems that had developed in the shadow of the ancient philosophies, and the forms of government that had molded Indian attitudes toward politics before the advent of British rule, while they were the objects of wide scholarship in England, received scant attention in continental Europe and the United States. By neglecting these realities and over-evaluating the religious and philosophical factors in Indian life and thought, an image was gradually fashioned of the Indian nation as essentially spiritual in its orientation and therefore righteous in its conduct.

This stereotype was not dislodged during India's struggle for independence. On the contrary, there is reason to believe that it was reenforced, especially in this country, by the new impression India made as a liberty-loving nation. For the objectives of

From Adda B. Bozeman, "India's Foreign Policy Today: Reflections on Its Sources," *World Politics*, 10 (January 1958), 256–263, 265–272, selections. Reprinted by permission.

the fight for freedom as well as the methods employed on its behalf were generally regarded in the West as ethically right, even though the issue of righteousness was being judged not in terms of Indian religion and philosophy — with which modern Indian nationalism has no connection — but in terms of Western liberalism — which is the spiritual anchorage for modern Indian movements toward liberty. Any discrepancy between the common Western conception of India and the Indian reality was thus covered up when India entered the society of established states and set out to create itself in its own image.

It takes a long time for a new state to gain a sense of its own identity, and it takes even longer for established states to identify the nature of the new state. For the evidence required for this type of recognition accumulates slowly as the new nation manifests itself in domestic and foreign affairs. It is therefore more difficult to interpret than that conventionally required for an assessment of the mere fact of statehood. Those in the West who thought they had recognized India's true identity before 1947 were somewhat disturbed by such early manifestations of the Indian state as New Delhi's approaches toward the problems of Kashmir and Hyderabad. But it took the United Nations debate in 1956–57 on Soviet aggression in Hungary to shake their confidence in the idea, to which they had consciously or unconsciously held fast, that India was a particularly righteous nation.

Now it is interesting to note that public opinion in India did not rally wholeheartedly behind the government's view of the nation's identity as expressed in its policy toward the Hungarian case. Several Indian writers and politicians were highly critical of their country's voting record in the United Nations, and something like a public debate on the merits of India's foreign policy seemed in the offing. Illustrative of the criticisms then voiced was that of Frank Moraes, the author of Mr. Nehru's biography, who wrote:

I must confess to a sense of acute embarrassment when India abstained in the General Assembly in November on the vote condemning Russia's action in Hungary, and to discomfiture and dismay when we actually opposed the proposal that the Soviet troops should be asked to withdraw from Hungary. Neither of these actions can be satisfactorily explained, certainly not by the devious technical pleas which Mr. Krishna Menon so combatively raised. . . .

Similar views were expressed elsewhere in the press. In fact, Mr. Nehru was politely taken to task for lecturing other nations in international ethics by expounding what T. S. Bawa has called the *Code de Nehru* in international relations, and for betraying this code in the conduct of his own nation's foreign policy. This public debate, if such it may be called, grew fainter when the Kashmir issue united Indians of all political opinion. It stopped altogether during the [1957] election, when the Prime Minister counseled the Bombay electorate to vote for Mr. Krishna Menon because he would regard the outcome of this particular vote as an approval or disapproval of his government's general stand in foreign affairs.

It is within this context that this study of the sources of contemporary Indian foreign policy was conducted. The conclusions reached will be presented here by outlining (1) several basic policy statements that the government has made officially; (2) actual policies that are discernible in the present-day record; and (3) the sources of reference that seem to determine Indian thought and action in the field of foreign affairs.

Certain guiding principles for the conduct of international relations were laid down by the Indian National Congress in 1920 and 1927. Resolutions were then passed to the effect that India would cooperate with other, especially neighboring, countries; that India would not become a party to an imperialist war; and that she would never join a war without the consent of her people. These principles were elaborated after 1947 largely through the mechanism of the Prime Minister's speeches —

Nehru speaks often, usually extemporaneously, and at great length — until they could be summarized in the now-familiar statement that India stands for "positive neutralism and nonalignment with major power blocs." Other official statements of policy goals are the Charter of the United Nations, to which India subscribed, and the so-called *panca sila*,[1] now the principal official reference in foreign affairs. These five precepts were set out in April 1954 in the preamble to the Sino-Indian Agreement on trade with Tibet. They were subsequently confirmed in a joint statement by Nehru and Chou En-lai, and have since been restated in numerous bilateral declarations made by India on the one hand, and Asian and Eastern European states, including the Soviet Union, on the other. The *panca sila*, which the Prime Minister has explained as India's answer to the doctrine of security pacts, lists these five norms of international behavior: (1) mutual respect for each other's territorial integrity and sovereignty; (2) nonaggression; (3) noninterference in each other's individual affairs; (4) equality and mutual advantage; and (5) peaceful coexistence and economic cooperation.

Within the framework of these and other verbalizations, the following actual policies or positions have become discernible:

(1) The incorporation of Kashmir. It should be noted, however, that in Indian opinion this is not a foreign-policy issue, for Kashmir is regarded today as an integral part of India.

(2) The retention of some degree of control over the foreign relations of neighboring Nepal.

(3) The promotion of the strength and solidarity of all Asia — indeed, of the entire non-Western world.

(4) The fight against colonialism and imperialism. The Indians — for that matter, most Asians — seem to define "imperialism" as any manner of control exercised by white over nonwhite nations. Frank Moraes elucidates this interpretation in the following passage:

> Quite frankly, the concept of Soviet imperialism or colonialism makes little impact on the Asian mind, which has always equated colonialism with colour. Colonialism, to Asia and Africa, spells the domination of white Powers over the coloured countries of the earth. The Japanese, it is true, were also condemned by India as colonialists in China. But pre-war Japan, according to the Asian thesis, was so wedded to Western techniques of production and power that her imperialism was a parallel projection on the political plane. Moreover, the traditional concept of colonialism fixes its main motivations in an urge for sources of cheap raw materials and for cheap and plentiful manpower.
>
> In Asian eyes no one of these tests applies to Soviet imperialism or colonialism. The countries behind the Iron Curtain are European and white with the exception of the Soviet Asian republics which claim to be equal and autonomous units of the U.S.S.R. Colour does not enter into this form of imperialism. . . . Nor are the Iron Curtain nations reservoirs of cheap manpower or sources of cheap raw materials. . . .

(5) Hostility to close political relations with any of the Western nations. The most recent manifestation of this attitude is India's growing alienation from Britain. The threat that India might leave the Commonwealth, which came originally from the extremists, notably the Communists, is now not discounted as a future possibility in Congress Party circles. This became evident in the Lok Sabha debates of March 1957, when the Commonwealth did not have many champions.

(6) Solicitation of foreign aid, notably from the United States and other Western nations. This goal is being pursued with increased vigor, for the second Five Year Plan counts on the receipt of Rp. crores 800 (1 cr. = 10 million) from foreign aid sources.

(7) The establishment of India as a great power. It is difficult not to agree with A. D. Gorwala when he writes:

[1] *"Panch Shila"* and *"Panchsheel"* are other variations. [Editor's note.]

Another significant influence on the minds
of the elite is what might be called the "great
power complex." The vastness of India and the
memory of its ancient glories arouse in them a
desire to embark on schemes that will appear
appreciable from contemporary . . . standards
anywhere in the world. Hence, forgetting
basic things, or regarding them as secondary,
they concentrate on grandiose attractions like
enormous buildings, huge international conferences, the pomp and outward paraphernalia
of governments, splendid representation in
foreign lands, luxury consumer services. . . .

Now it cannot be said that these policies
are consistent in all instances with the
guiding principles as they have been officially stated. Nor can it be said that all of
these policies are mutually compatible. For
example, while India claims to be neutral
in the great controversies of the day — can
a nation that has great-power aspirations
ever be neutral in international relations?
— she has in fact shown herself partial to
the totalitarian regimes when they were
ranged against democratic governments.
This point has been made rather emphatically by Frank Moraes:

The one criticism, however, which can be
made against our policy of non-alignment is
not that it is unsuited to the needs of our
country or unrealistic, but that in implementing it we have often laid ourselves open to
the charge that we are inclined more in favor
of the totalitarian countries such as Russia and
China than of the democracies. The complaint is often heard — and I personally feel it
is legitimate — that in cases where we might
have given the benefit of the doubt to the
democracies, we have chosen to give it to the
totalitarian countries.

A further manifestation of partiality is the
steady support, undifferentiated by consideration of objective issues, which India has
given to Asian and African nations in their
relations with those of Europe and America.
It can be argued, in fact, that the Bandung
alliance itself is an "alignment" with one of
the major world powers, i.e., China.

If one examines the policies that are designed to promote the solidarity of all Asia,

the sovereign equality of all nonwhite nations, and India's own prestige as a great
power, one finds several other striking
inconsistencies. The most obvious violation
of the spirit of Bandung is surely India's
bitter enmity toward her Asian neighbor,
Pakistan. And one may also refer, in this
context, to the condescension with which
India treats Nepal, and to those cracks and
fissures in India's common front with Ceylon and Burma, which are due primarily to
the distrust in which India's great-power
aspirations are held by the weaker nations
of the region.

Lastly, one may doubt the logic of a foreign policy that seeks to procure economic
assistance on a vast scale from the Western
democracies and at the same time persists in
discriminating openly against these nations.

Now it may be interjected at this point
that the proper test of a policy is not its
inner logic but its total external success in
promoting the economic and political security of the state. But how successful is
India's foreign policy in these respects? The
record discussed here indicates that the twin
causes of neutrality and Asian solidarity
have not been furthered appreciably in the
past years. And while India has thus far
been successful in bolstering her economic
security by eliciting aid from the West, she
has come dangerously close to exhausting
the tremendous reservoir of good-will which
has released the flow of economic assistance
in the past. But the chief failure of India's
foreign policy was registered in the realm
of political security, when China succeeded
in driving a hard bargain in the matter of
Tibet, the *panca sila* notwithstanding; for
India was then forced to acquiesce in a
political arrangement that implied the for-
feiture of long-standing strategic advantages
on the all-important northern frontier.

These and other incongruities, ambigu-
ities, and failures have not been explained
either by the Indian government or by Indian critics of the political scene. Indeed, a
Western student of Indian politics cannot
help but register amazement at the ease
with which conflicting arguments and ref-

erences are accepted by even the most informed section of the Indian public. In the absence of any Indian lead in this respect, it is therefore perhaps not too presumptuous for an outsider to inquire into the sources that determine or explain Indian attitudes toward the conduct of international relations.

The foreign policy of any modern state devolves from implied or explicit references to strategic, economic, and ideological considerations, and aims at the preservation and furtherance of the national interest. But the conceptual sources and political definitions of the national interest vary from country to country, as do the meanings and emphases given to the factors that influence its determination. The Indian government has been less outspoken than most other governments in defining the national interest in strategic terms, but even a cursory glance at India's northern boundary will convince an observer that considerations of military security must be a primary concern in New Delhi. This impression is borne out by the actual measures that have been taken in order to repress the revolts of the Naga Hostiles[2] and to keep the peace in Bhutan, Sikkim, and Assam, and by the obvious and understandable, but not openly admitted, Indian interest in controlling the strategically vital valley of Kashmir.

That India's national interest is wound up inextricably with its economic development goes without saying. Although this connection has not been made explicit whenever the government has explained its foreign policies to the public, it has been stressed by the Prime Minister when he has had occasion to theorize about the essence of all foreign policy. A speech he delivered on December 4, 1947, at the Constituent Assembly in New Delhi, contains the following passage: "Ultimately, foreign policy is the outcome of economic policy, and un-til India has properly evolved her economic policy, her foreign policy will be rather vague, rather inchoate, and will be groping."

Most foreign policy statements since 1947 have been presented in deliberately political and ideological terms. It seems justifiable, therefore, to focus this inquiry upon the intellectual sources of India's present foreign policy.

A survey of India's long history leads to the conclusion that contemporary political thought is caught in a welter of different and contradictory intellectual references that have been derived in successive stages from Hinduism, Buddhism, Islam, Western liberalism, and Marxism-Leninism. It is the predicament of the present generation of political theorists and statesmen that they must identify and evaluate each of these references in terms of its political content, and reconcile conflicting intellectual positions, before they can hope to find an overall orientation that would both meet the practical problems of the twentieth century and still accord with those traditions that are found to have an enduring hold on the Indian mind. This predicament has not yet been recognized in India. . . .

The question, then, is, to what intellectual context does the government refer its policies? The policy statements that were reviewed earlier point rather obviously to Buddhist ethics, citing as the principal platform of India's present foreign policy the so-called *panca sila*. It is important, therefore, for the purposes of this discussion, to examine the relationship of Buddhist ethics to Indian foreign policy.

The system of Buddhist ethics as originally formulated had nothing to do with political ideologies. Its purpose was the development of a nonpolitical mentality, withdrawn from the concerns of acquisitive and self-defensive action. With this end in mind the Buddha laid down Ten Precepts or Commandments, the first five of which were to be regarded as the fundamental moral code by brethren and laymen alike (the other five were binding only on the

[2] The Nagas are a tribal people in the northeastern region of India, some of whom have violently resisted political integration. [Editor's note.]

monks). These five precepts — the *panca sila* — admonished the Buddhist to avoid (1) the destruction of life, (2) theft, (3) unchastity, (4) lying, and (5) the use of intoxicating liquor. They constitute the central part of the content of Buddhist morality as taught and practiced today over the entire Buddhist world. Now, it is important in connection with this inquiry to recall the fact that an attempt was made in the reign of Asoka, himself a devout Buddhist, to introduce Buddhist ethics into international relations. The attempt failed — in fact, it was conducive to the disintegration of Asoka's empire. Without entering into the merits of the question whether Buddhism can ever be transformed into a political ideology governing the conduct of states and still retain its character as a religion of individual salvation, let us see what is actually involved in the evocation of Buddhist ethics in twentieth-century Asian, especially Indian and Chinese, politics.

Firstly, it must be remembered that Buddhism has long ceased to be a frame of reference for individual conduct in both India and China — the two nations that discovered the *panca sila* as the governing principle in their foreign relations.

Secondly, it is obvious from the biographies of the two leading statesmen — Nehru and Chou En-lai — that both are far removed in their thoughts and actions not only from Buddhism but also from any other religion.

And, thirdly, it is difficult indeed to find any relationship whatsoever between the *panca sila* as formulated by Nehru and Chou En-lai, and the *panca sila* of the Buddhist religion. In other words, the reference to Buddhist ethics in the context of Indian foreign policy is spurious.

The true provenance of the concepts contained in Mr. Nehru's *panca sila* — namely, mutual respect for each other's territory, nonaggression, noninterference in each other's internal affairs, equality and mutual advantage, and peaceful coexistence and economic cooperation — is the modern history of international organization as developed in the Western world. For each and all of these principles of international conduct are not only embodied in the Charter of the United Nations, but may be found also in many documents that preceded this international constitution. Such an acknowledgment could not be expected in the prevailing climate of opinion; and even if it had been forthcoming, it would have been unreasonable to assume that India's interpretation of the concepts would have been in accord with Western traditions. But what is disconcerting here is the realization that few Indians today actually perceive the parallel between their "new" statement of policy on the one hand, and the old political tradition of the West on the other.

Now, this was different in the less self-conscious days of India's movement toward independence, when the nation's intellectual leadership frankly acknowledged the validity, for India's foreign policy, of the cultural context in which such preferred values as national independence, self-government, and sovereignty had been developed — witness the resolutions of the Congress in 1920 and 1927, discussed earlier. Indeed, it was Gandhi's imaginative and original reading and use of the literary, philosophical, and religious traditions of the West which accounts, to a considerable extent, for the apt formulation of the concept of nonviolence in international relations. It is true that this policy was actually applied only to India's relations with the British, and its singular success is therefore no proof of its intrinsic value or wisdom. Nevertheless, a significant new reference for the conduct of international relations had been found, and it is proper to ask, therefore, whether the principle of nonviolence has been accommodated in post-Gandhian India, and, if so, in what form.

Few aspects of the intellectual history of the independence movement are as interesting and significant as the relationship between Gandhi and Nehru. In fact, it is possible to read this history as a continuous

dialogue between two outstanding person-
alities who viewed the great problems of
life in general, and of their nation in particular, in very different ways. Their biographies make it clear that Nehru could not
accede to a philosophy that glorified the
nation's poverty and stressed the importance
on nonpolitical activities, and that he could
not understand or appreciate the older
man's insistence on nonviolence as a cardinal principle of political behavior. The
choice between violence and nonviolence
was to be determined in Nehru's view by
practical, not by moral, considerations. In
1929 he condoned the tactic of nonviolence
on the ground that resort to violence, far
from promising substantial results in the
struggle for freedom, would have been conducive to the disruption of the nation.
After 1947 Mr. Nehru saw the problem
differently, for his government did not hesitate to resort to armed force in Hyderabad
and Kashmir. One must thus agree with
Moraes when he writes that India has no
doctrinaire attachment to the concept of
nonviolence.

If India's present foreign policy is not
anchored in Indian systems of thought,
where are its ideological roots? The answer,
derived from a study of recorded political
pronouncements and actions, points clearly
to the Marxist-Leninist theory of history
and economics as it was expounded at the
London School of Economics in the 1920's
and 1930's, and as it was understood by
Nehru personally. This body of references,
which was not accepted by Motilal Nehru,
Gandhi, and other older leaders of the Congress, impressed Jawaharlal Nehru as a
dynamic set of principles and as a call to
action. It illumined his reading of world
history, his interpretation of India's experiences under British rule, his pessimistic
analysis of Europe's problems, and his optimistic view of all developments in the
Soviet Union. The principal theoretical
propositions appropriated by Mr. Nehru
from this source are: that the European
concept of democracy is a shell cloaking
great inequalities and that it is apt to become perverted in terms of facism; that
capitalism provides its own grave diggers;
that capitalism is the head and fount of the
vicious sin of colonialism; that its spawn,
imperialism, nurtures within itself the seeds
of conflict and decay; and that socialism as
implemented in the Soviet Union holds
out the greatest hope in this dismal age.
Two excerpts from Mr. Nehru's writings
are illustrative of these views. In a letter
to his daughter[3] he writes: "Fascism thus
appears when the class conflicts between
an advancing socialism and an entrenched
capitalism become bitter and critical. . . .
So long as capitalism can use the machinery
of democratic institutions to hold power
and keep down labour, democracy is allowed to flourish. When this is not possible,
then capitalism discards democracy and
adopts the open Fascist method of violence
and terror."

And in his book *Toward Freedom,*
Nehru expounds this thesis in the following terms:

Two rival economic and political systems faced
each other in the world, and, though they
tolerated each other for a while, there was an
inherent antagonism between them, and they
played for mastery on the stage of the world.
One of them was the capitalist order, which
had *inevitably* developed into vast imperial-
isms, which, having swallowed the colonial
world, were intent on eating each other up.
Powerful still and fearful of war, which might
endanger their possessions, yet they came into
inevitable conflict with each other and prepared feverishly for war. They were quite
unable to solve the problems that threatened
them, and helplessly they submitted to slow
decay. The other was the new socialist order
of the U.S.S.R., which went from progress to
progress, though often at terrible cost, and
where the problems of the capitalist world had
ceased to exist.

Capitalism, in its difficulties, took to fascism with all its brutal suppression of what
Western civilization had apparently stood for;

---

[3] Indira Nehru, later Mrs. Indira Nehru Gandhi
(but no relation to Mahatma Gandhi), who became India's Prime Minister in 1966. [Editor's
note.]

it became, even in some of its homelands, what its imperialist counterpart had long been in the subject colonial countries. Fascism and imperialism thus stood out as the two faces of the now decaying capitalism . . . they represented the same forces of reaction and supported each other, and at the same time came into conflict with each other, for such conflict was inherent in their very nature. Socialism in the West and rising nationalisms of the Eastern and other dependent countries opposed this combination of fascism and imperialism. Nationalism in the East, it must be remembered, was essentially different from the new and terribly narrow nationalism of the fascist countries; the former was the historical urge to freedom, the latter the last refuge to reaction.

To the question where India should stand, Nehru answered that "Inevitably we take our stand with the progressive forces of the world which are ranged against fascism and imperialism."

The affinities between Mr. Nehru's application of the Leninist formula of Marxism to world politics and that expounded by Harold Laski in the 1930's and 1940's are striking. For Laski, too, was convinced that the capitalist democracies would "inevitably" degenerate into fascism. Indeed, he maintained that the Fascist state is, "nakedly and without shame, what the state, covertly and apologetically is, in capitalist democracies like Great Britain or the United States," and that the distinction between the judicial systems of capitalist democracies and of Fascist dictatorships is one of degree rather than of kind. The only possibilities, Laski concluded, are therefore the opposite alternatives of fascism and revolutionary socialism. Like Nehru, Laski pointed continuously to the sharp contrast between the spirit of exhilaration and optimism found in the Soviet Union and the general sense of insecurity and anxiety found in capitalist countries. Both men were convinced that the Soviet Union held out the highest hope for a regeneration of mankind, and both were immensely impressed with the capacity of communism to arouse mass enthusiasm. But neither has ever wanted to identify himself completely with

the cause of communism. Their writings indicate that they were irritated by the methods which the Communists employed in the furtherance of their aims and that they preferred the means of effecting change that had been perfected in the Western democracies. But while Laski dropped this preference gradually, Nehru has continued to insist that Marxist blueprints can be executed by democratic means. For example, in accounting for his participation in the Congress of Oppressed Nationalities held in Brussels in 1927–28, he has admitted that he usually sided with the Anglo-Americans on questions of methods even though he shared the objectives pursued by the Communists. Indeed, Nehru's entire approach to government as the practical agency for reforming society reflects strongly the influence of English constitutionalism. That India is still a democracy — however hollow this form of government is made to appear in Mr. Nehru's theories — is, as a matter of fact, largely due to the Prime Minister's insistence on maintaining democratic processes at home.

The contradiction between Mr. Nehru's approach to government and his interpretation of international relations has never been resolved. It is nowhere more apparent than in his attitude toward the Communist Party. For while he approves of what the Party stands for in the context of world politics, he evidently does not like it as a political phenomenon. Indeed, he goes out of his way in trying to separate the Party and its international activities from the policies which Communist nations pursue.

These assumptions, implicit in Mr. Nehru's mode of thinking, seem to have become immovable fixtures in the official Indian system of political references. No one in authority has questioned their intrinsic validity in the light of the many political and economic changes that have occurred in the Western democracies and the Soviet orbit during the last twenty years. Nothing in the development of the United States seems to have shaken the thesis that America is a capitalist country in the doctrinaire sense of the word, and therefore imperialistic by definition. Nothing in the evolution of Russian communism seems to have suggested to Mr. Nehru close analogies to Fascist totalitarianism, and nothing in the expansion of the Soviet Union seems to have reminded him of the phenomenon of imperialism as he had defined it in his younger days.

The survival of this stereotyped set of intellectual references in world affairs, which stands in marked contrast to the resourceful and imaginative use of ideas in Indian domestic politics, is due primarily to the fact that foreign policy matters are generally regarded in India as falling within the exclusive competence of the Prime Minister, whereas domestic issues are constantly reviewed and reappraised by India's numerous democratic institutions. In these circumstances it is only Mr. Nehru personally who could have scrutinized the basic assumption of his approach to inter-national relations. Such a scrutiny has not been forthcoming, for reasons that appear clearly in Mr. Nehru's written and oral pronouncements. These biographical records reveal that the Prime Minister is a man of very strong feelings, and that two emotions in particular have dominated his thoughts about foreign affairs: a deep hostility to the West and an unshakeable faith in everything Asian. And these emotional commitments became irrevocable when it was found that they could be vindicated by certain rational propositions implicit in the dogma of Marxism-Leninism. In other words, it was the seeming concurrence of emotionally and rationally held truths which provided the Prime Minister with a formula for the analysis of international relations. And it is this Indian formula which supplies the key to an understanding of the inconsistencies that the non-Indian, non-Marxist observer finds so puzzling in India's approach to foreign affairs. . . .

Defects in Practice

J. B. KRIPALANI

Since the Tibetan crisis of 1950, J. B. Kripalani, an independent Gandhian and a former Congress party president, has been a leading critic of selected aspects of Indian foreign policy. As shown in this reading, he fully approves of many of the ideals and objectives of nonalignment announced by the Indian government and its supporters. What disturbs him is the relation of principles to practice in specific emergencies and Prime Minister Nehru's China policy between 1950 and 1959. A many-sided commentator who has stimulated debates in the Indian Parliament and was reelected in the 1967 General Elections, Kripalani interprets communism differently than do progressive Indian nationalists and his views of economic development conflict with those of the country's policy makers. His position within the Gandhian stream of Indian nationalism and his established reputation as a nonconformist make him one of the more creative interpreters of nonalignment.

In the present international circumstances, India, following her basic principles, has taken a position of nonalignment or neutrality as between the two power blocs, the Western and the Russian. But the Prime Minister of India has often said that Indian neutrality is not passive but dynamic. He means that India will freely express her opinion in international affairs and show her sympathy and solidarity with victims of aggression and injustice.

In spite of the fact that Independent India was new to international diplomacy, her prestige in international affairs was somehow high, especially among Asio-African nations. This was due in part to the size of her territory, her geographical position and her vast population. It was also due to the unique character of the Indian struggle for independence, which put confidence and courage in colonial peoples everywhere by demonstrating that even an unarmed nation, if determined, could win its freedom. It was further felt that both before and after independence India's basic principles were just and human. Though Western democracies mouthed the same principles, they were suspect, since they still held in an iron grip the remnants of their empires. The United States was not imperial in the West European sense, but it was thought to desire domination of other nations through its economic power. Its good faith was further suspect because of its alliances with imperialistic democracies and with non-Communist totalitarian and military régimes whose actions it could not control. The doctrine recently enunciated by President Eisenhower of "filling the vacuum" created by the dwindling influences of England and France in West Asia caused further distrust of American political motives. Both in Korea and Indochina the Western nations supported what Asians considered reactionary régimes. Naturally, therefore, Asio-African nations looked to free India for sympathy, support and guidance. Their representatives in the United Nations often consulted their Indian colleagues before making up their minds about policy decisions.

From J. B. Kripalani, "For Principled Neutrality," *Foreign Affairs*, 38 (October 1959), 47–52, selections. Reprinted by permission.

India's prestige in international affairs was enhanced when it was offered, and accepted, the chairmanship of international commissions appointed after the deadlock in Korea and Indochina. The big powers which had indirectly come to grips in these two regions knew that any further fighting might lead to a third world war. They found a way out by consenting to cease-fire agreements on the basis of the status quo and the appointment of international commissions to solve immediate problems. But they were not willing to play the game to bring about peace in these countries and their ultimate unification. The international commissions formed under Indian chairmanship therefore could not discharge their responsibilities effectively and in course of time they seem to have faded away.

Indian prestige was further enhanced when an Indian, a woman at that, was elected President of the United Nations General Assembly.[1] It was not generally realized that, owing to the jealousies and rivalries of the big powers, this position of prestige without power could go only to prominent politicians in militarily weak countries.

Whatever may have been the failings of the Congress Party government in internal affairs, it could always with some justification show that it had added to the prestige and standing of India in the international world. But all this prestige did not advance any vital interests of India or diminish tension on her borders. Our relations with Pakistan are as strained as ever. The Kashmir issue remains internationally confused. In the case of the tiny Portuguese imperial possessions in India, no progress has been made; indeed the situation has deteriorated. On her northern frontier, India allowed the annihilation of the buffer kingdom of Tibet without a protest; we have recognized the legitimacy of the Chinese claim there. The question of the citizenship of Indian nationals domiciled for decades in Ceylon still hangs fire. There is no improvement in our relations with South Africa.

Why is this so? It is because the Indian Government thought that the whole business of diplomacy consisted in enunciating the principles of international policy. But international politics is not concerned merely with enunciation of abstract principles. It is very much concerned with international diplomacy, strategy and tactics. To use the old metaphor, it will not do to lose sight of the trees in contemplating the beauty of the forest, for it is the trees, after all, which yield useful fruit and timber. To take a historical example: President Wilson during World War I enunciated important moral and political principles to regulate international affairs, but after the war his weak diplomatic strategy failed and paved the way to World War II.

It is true that the international complications which faced India, and still face her today, especially on her borders, are not of her creation. They are historical legacies. But what is successful diplomacy? It is not that a country should enjoy international prestige, desirable as that may be, but that it should be able to safeguard its vital interests, without recourse to war. At least it should be able to reduce tensions. Successful diplomacy should counteract the adverse effects of historical circumstances.

Another condition of successful diplomacy is to take appropriate action at the proper time. In politics, national or international, opportunities once missed are generally missed for good, or at least do not rise again in the same favorable form. The nation which fails to take advantage of a favorable opportunity has often to pay the full price of its mistakes, even as the merchant must for his miscalculated deals. The law of *Karma*[2] is inexorable.

Let us take the example of the China-

---

[1] Mrs. Vijaya Lakshmi Pandit, a sister of Nehru, who has served as India's Ambassador to the Soviet Union and the United States and Governor of Maharashtra state. [Editor's note.]

[2] Hinduism's concept of spiritual debt which individuals must erase to end the cycle of rebirths. [Editor's note.]

Tibet conflict. In resolution after resolution, the Indian National Congress before and after independence had denounced the domination of one nation over another. India never recognized unjust historical claims. If she had, her own struggle for independence would have had little justification. So it was, then, that immediately after independence when we invited to our country a conference of Asian countries, Tibet was included as a free nation. When the so-called Chinese liberation army marched into Tibet our government rightly protested. In surprise our Prime Minister asked: "From whom is Tibet to be liberated?" For this protest, Communist China dubbed us "the running dogs of imperialism." I am afraid we yielded to the usual Communist bullying tactics and allowed China a free hand in Tibet. Perhaps we were misinformed by our representative there about the nature of Chinese Communism.[3] However that may be, we had no right to give our conscience a sop by taking refuge under the historic right of suzerainty claimed by Communist China. This suzerainty, as we know, or as students of history we ought to have known, was imposed upon Tibet by powerful imperial countries but was never accepted by the people or rulers of Tibet.

The question often asked is, what could India have done? We could not possibly go to war on this issue; but the alternative to war is not acquiescence in injustice. We denounced the aggression of Britain, France and Israel against Egypt, but this did not involve us in war. Today we side with the Algerian struggle for independence, but this has not meant the cutting of our normal and friendly relations with France. Acquiescence in aggression amounts to appeasement, which merely whets the appetite of the aggressor, as was seen at the time of Munich. England was not prepared for war with Hitler. But Chamberlain's mistake was to acquiesce in

Hitler's aggression against Czechoslovakia by declaring it a distant country about which the English people knew little. In the case of China, we could have recognized the *de facto* Communist rule on Chinese soil and continued diplomatic and trade relations with the new government. We have such relations with France in spite of Algeria and with Russia in spite of Hungary. We have them with England even though she has not freed all her colonies. We have not ceased to be a member of the British Commonwealth, though some of its members are not friendly to us and indulge in racial discrimination against us. It is usual to recognize *de facto* governments, within their own borders, whatever their origin. However, when the means used to acquire power are of a doubtful character, the *de facto* and the *de jure* recognition should not be accorded immediately, especially the latter. One must wait and see if the new régime is accepted by the bulk of the people, without undue coercion. It was not even amiss to advocate the cause of Communist China's membership in the United Nations. It would not have been the first or only imperialist power represented in that august body. But we should never have put the seal of our approval on the rape of a virtually independent nation. India herself renounced her extraterritorial rights over Tibet, acquired under British imperial rule. We renounced these rights because we believed in the freedom of nations in spite of historical accidents to the contrary. India did not renounce these rights in favor of China but of Tibet. Even though we were assured that, unlike Soviet Russia, Communist China was democratic and progressive, we should have known that a régime that insists on unjust historical rights, derived from previous governments which it considered imperialist and reactionary, cannot be liberal or progressive. In their international affairs the Communist régimes in both Russia and China follow the expansionist and imperialist policies of the Tsars and of the Chinese emperors and Chiang Kai-shek.

[3] The reference is to K. M. Panikkar, India's Ambassador to China during the 1950 Tibetan crisis. [Editor's note.]

In any case, by 1954, when the treaty between India and China was signed, the character of this régime was, or should have been, clear to the Indian Government. Yet by that treaty we confirmed the suzerainty of China. Since 1950, mine has been the solitary voice raised in the Indian Parliament against the recognition of the suzerainty of China over Tibet and in favor of Tibetan independence. Speaking in the House in 1958 on *Panchsheel*, I said that it "was born in sin in as much as by it we put the seal of our approval on the annihilation of a free nation." Subsequent tragic events have justified my criticism. Our recognition of Chinese suzerainty over Tibet is in clear contradiction to what our Prime Minister has often said: "Where freedom is menaced or justice threatened, or where aggression takes place, we cannot and shall not be neutral." This is dynamic neutrality. In the case of Tibet we have not been even neutral. We have dynamically sided with the aggressor.

. . . There is always a danger in overemphasizing moral and ideological principles in international affairs. There are bound to be contradictions in the actual conduct of nations in dealing with each other. Our Prime Minister is never tired of repeating that "War solves no problems." Yet the expenditure on the Indian Army has been progressively increasing. As I once said in the Indian Parliament, supposing Pakistan was foolish enough to attack India, or if today China did so, would India fight? If she did, it would mean war. Would such a war be fought by India in the belief that war solves no problems? Armies are not maintained or military expenses incurred or wars undertaken on the assumption that war solves no problems. Rather the assumption is that, as long as the world has found no peaceful way of redressing international wrongs, war, in the last resort, is the only way of vindicating international justice and maintaining national dignity and independence. Today no nation maintaining an army which swallows a large part of its revenues,

sometimes 50 per cent and more, can with any logic or honesty hold that war solves no problems.

We also often say that the cold war is the result of fear. This is true. But we cannot talk too often of it, if we ourselves are afraid of Pakistan and of China. We cannot make light of the Russian fear of the United States, or vice versa. Even more, we cannot blame the Western European nations if they are afraid of Russia or if today the Asian nations fear expansionist China. Military power even for defense is born of fear. Only a determined nation, believing in nonviolence, prepared for annihilation but unwilling to yield to injustice and tyranny, can really be fearless. This is what Gandhiji taught us, and he was right. It is no use reminding other nations of the faults from which we ourselves are not immune. Moral platitudes can be mouthed by politicians once in a while, but if they are repeated frequently, without appropriate action, their authors cannot escape the charge of hypocrisy.

For instance, the United States claims that if it ever goes to war against Communist powers it will be in defense of democracy and the free world. Do we believe these high and altruistic assertions when in pursuit of them the United States enters into alliances with imperialists and dictators? Would it not be better for the United States to say that it wants to safeguard its national freedom and is afraid of the expansionist designs of the Soviet Union? In that case, alliances with military dictators and imperialists to strengthen itself, however opportunistic, will not look so incongruous and hypocritical as they do today. If we are reluctant to believe in the pious utterances of others, we may be sure that such utterances by us, unsupported by appropriate action, will not be believed. Repeated platitudes will only confirm the belief, now so general, that the words of politicians have no meaning. They are blub, blub, blub. If words have no meaning, communication becomes difficult.

Take again the *Panchsheel*. Its principles if analyzed would amount to maintaining the status quo in international affairs, however inequitable. Neither the aggrieved nations nor the aggressor nations want or can maintain this status quo. For instance, there can be no peaceful coexistence between nations which have diametrically opposite apostolic missions to discharge and which want to do it through violence, war and crooked diplomacy. Nor can a conquered nation consent to peaceful coexistence with its imperial masters of whatever hue. Algeria can have no peaceful coexistence with France, nor for that matter can the Arab nations. Hungary cannot live in a state of peaceful coexistence with Russia or Tibet with China. The Portuguese dictator [Salazar] takes refuge under the *Panchsheel* doctrine of peaceful coexistence to deny the right of India in Goa or of the inhabitants thereof. Peaceful coexistence in such cases will be that of the lamb with lion, when the lamb is safe in its belly.

The same applies to other principles of *Panchsheel*. One cannot respect the sovereignty of imperial nations over their colonies, yet international law recognizes it as a fact. The independence of nations must be recognized and realized before there can be peaceful coexistence or mutual respect of each other's sovereignty. The *Panchsheel* principles are not moral imperatives that can be adhered to unilaterally. In international affairs, even moral principles have no unilateral application; much less can *Panchsheel*, which depends upon mutuality of rights and obligations. It is therefore no wonder that recently while on a visit to Nepal the Indian Prime Minister when questioned about *Panchsheel* was constrained to say, in effect, "Where is *Panchsheel?* It cannot be worked in the present international situation. It has become merely a slogan."

When all nations believe in war, in the ultimate, as the solvent of international problems, there is something to be said in favor of the doctrine of "brinkmanship," enunciated by the late Secretary of State, Mr. Dulles. As a matter of fact this is no new doctrine. It has been enunciated by politicians everywhere when they say, "Believe in God but keep your powder dry." On the basis of violence, no other kind of diplomacy is likely to succeed.

Unfortunately most nations have not powder enough to keep dry. It is also true that even the most powerful nation today cannot defend itself singlehandedly. It is therefore natural for nations to enter into military alliances for mutual protection. But there are countries which enter these alliances not for the purposes of defense but to safeguard their imperial interests or work their designs on their neighbors. For instance, Pakistan, as she has often said, has only one enemy — India. But for India, she would be neutral like most of the Asiatic countries which have recently achieved independence. France uses the military help she receives from the United States against Algeria. Portugal is in NATO to safeguard her imperial possessions. But in the confused international world of today this is inevitable, when both parties to the cold war want to strengthen themselves by any alliance, however doubtful.

It nevertheless is good that, in spite of any strength they might gain from military alliances, some nations have chosen to remain neutral. They do so for valid and weighty reasons. Not only do they have no expansionist designs, but they also feel that if they ally themselves with more powerful nations, and especially if they allow them military bases (ultimately it will come to that), they will impair their independence. Further, they believe that if more nations are linked in military alliances there is a greater danger of world conflagration, which, with the present nuclear weapons, may destroy humanity. If the number of neutral nations increases there will be a greater possibility of settling international problems through negotiations and conferences, below or at the summit. It will also mean more and more reliance on the good offices of the United Nations, thereby strengthening that organization. Even as it is, its services are utilized when the rival big powers feel that any further fighting in which they are directly or indirectly involved, if not speedily stopped, will produce complications leading to world war. This happened in Korea and Indochina and during the Suez and other West Asian troubles. In any case, regional military pacts weaken the standing and authority of the United Nations.

The underdeveloped Asio-African countries which have recently achieved freedom have so many political, economic and social problems of their own that they feel they must confine their attention to the solution of these rather than dabble in partisan international politics. They do not want to annoy any of the big powers. Furthermore, nations which have recently cast off the Western yoke are not quite sure that the colonialists have altogether abandoned the idea of regaining their old dominant position, given the opportunity. They therefore utilize the anti-imperialist assertions of Russia to keep in check fresh ambitions of the West. At the same time they are not enamored of the political and economic setup in Communist Russia or China. They therefore remain neutral. Further, they do not believe in the apostolic mission of reforming the world that both sides claim for themselves, one more fanatically and more aggressively than the other. No nation has been commissioned by God or His substitute, Historical Necessity, to reform the world.

These are good reasons for neutrality as between the two blocs, and they appeal to India. Therefore the policy of the Indian Government in this respect is generally accepted by the nation.

But with all these advantages, there is no guarantee of noninterference, direct or indirect, by the power blocs if they feel that their real of fancied interests are affected. Under these circumstances the neutrality of uncommitted nations can be useful to themselves and to the world only if it is born of strength of conviction and not out of weakness or opportunist considerations. In the latter case they cannot stick to it under strain from one side or the other. Their moral influence can count only when they refuse to yield to the threats and bullying tactics of powerful nations. There must be no compromise on clear issues, involving questions of international justice and peace. It must be understood that no nation can keep intact its independence and whatever moral influence it has without taking risks. To suppose that right conduct, whether in the individual or the group, involves no risks is not true to the facts of life and historical experience. As we have said, the risks involved in appeasement in the long run are greater. Where physical resistance is not possible, one must not shrink from moral resistance to evil. That is the only way to save one's liberty and self-respect. Unfortunately, the world is so constituted that right conduct does not save one from material loss and suffering. In the struggle for independence, even though it was nonviolent, India had to take great risks at critical times; and she did not hesitate to take them. Neutral nations have to resist the temptation of inclining to one side or the other to gain temporary advantage. They must be impartial. They must avoid any action which may undermine the confidence of other nations in their neutrality and do everything that will strengthen it.

It is natural that India should want to be friendly towards her Communist neighbors. Neighbors are most likely to have conflicting interests and to find ready cause for a fight. In Europe, West and East, I have been told by every country that it was friendly to India. My reply usually was: "Why not? We are not neighbors." That India should be anxious for friendship with Communist Russia and China, in spite of difference in ideology, should not be difficult to understand; but this anxiety should not blind us to whatever they say or do, particularly where the freedom and interests of other nations are concerned. For instance, our condemnation of Russian action in Hungary in 1956 was so halting and belated that it lost its merit. We were more forthright in condemning British, French and Israeli action in Egypt, and also American and British action in West Asia, when troops were landed in Lebanon and Jordan. In the case of Tibet as I said earlier, our attitude from the beginning has been in contradiction with our avowed principles. It has had the appearance of weakness and opportunism, of purchasing Chinese friendship at the cost of Tibet.

On occasions, we have allowed our guests from Communist countries to denounce Western democracies, with whom we are on friendly terms, from our soil. We cannot stop nations from denouncing each other. But if they do so they must do it from their own country and not from ours. It is possible for nations so attacked to feel that we share the views of our guests. In any case, they naturally feel aggrieved.

In assessing historical events, we should not forget contemporary facts. Whatever the world has suffered and is suffering from overseas imperialism, we cannot ignore the fact that, for whatever reasons or on whatever pretext, a new variety of imperialism has made its appearance. It nibbles at its neighbors and swallows them. It waits for some time, brief or long according to circumstances, to pounce on other victims. It has not the merit of being democratic even at home. In a Western country the existence of democracy at home mitigates to some extent the rigors of its domination in colonial lands. In England, Labor as a party, and some of its leaders individually, advocated democratic reforms in India. Ultimately, the Labor Party not only supported the cause of Indian independence but negotiated on that basis. In Communist countries there can be no vocal public opinion against their aggression or tyranny. Not a single voice was raised or could be raised in Communist Russia or China against the aggression in Hungary or Tibet and the atrocities committed in these hapless and helpless lands. Within democratic France there is a section of socialists and the whole bloc of Communists who advocate Algerian independence. (In non-Communist countries, the Communists, though

not very ardent patriots, are always the most passionate advocates of civil liberties and the freedom of the colonial peoples.) In the imperialist democracies, usually, when civil liberties are denied to colonial people or there is executive tyranny, some groups or individuals in parliament protest and rouse public opinion. This does not and cannot happen under dictatorships — Fascist, Communist or military. In the colonies of Western democracies, also, the legal system is generally modelled on the pattern of democracy at home, which affords some protection against executive highhandedness and tyranny. The legal system in totalitarian countries or their dependencies affords the individual no protection against political and executive highhandedness.

Toward the danger of this new imperialism the Indian attitude has not been as strong and unequivocal as it was toward the older imperialism from which India herself suffered. The old imperialism is thoroughly discredited and is on the decline. It no longer gets support from progressives and intellectuals even in imperialist countries. This does not mean that it does not weigh heavily on those who suffer from it. But the new Communist imperialism, now fast beginning to show its paws and claws, is more dangerous. It embraces in its vise both the home country and the dependencies. Moreover, it is imposed in the name of high principles and noble ends which may have an appeal for many intellectuals and idealists the world over.

As matters stand today, a neutral nation cannot afford to lean heavily on large loans from outside for the development of its internal economy, if it wants to maintain its independence of opinion and action. The anxiety for large loans has sometimes put India in an awkward position. Often when our representatives have gone to the West, especially to America, they have impressed upon their audiences the idea that if large loans are not advanced to India she will be overwhelmed by Communism; the great bastion of democracy in Asia will thus be destroyed. This appears to be a humiliating position for a great nation to take. If Communism is bad, India must resist, loans or no loans. Unarmed India did not rely on foreign powers or foreign financial aid in order to win its independence. Today it cannot rely upon huge foreign loans to meet not only its economic needs but also an internal Communist danger. Furthermore, Western nations understandably do not appreciate our criticizing them, even on issues which do not adversely affect our vital interests, at the same time that we ask them for large loans. An independent nation which wants to maintain its right to free criticism and action will do best to rely upon its own resources for its economic development.

To sum up, then, the principles upon which the Indian foreign policy of nonalignment is based are correct. They are generally accepted by the country and are in keeping with the genius of our people. If more nations will accept the same attitude there will be a definite lessening of international tension. It is in details of diplomacy that our foreign policy has been weak and has sometimes gone wrong. Our mistakes have to some extent impaired our moral standing as a neutral nation and have often injured our interests in various ways. But, after all, India is new to diplomacy, and the world situation is extremely complicated.

Misconceptions of International Politics

WERNER LEVI

Some critics of India's foreign policy hold that it depends on faulty appraisals of world politics. This charge probes the foundations of India's independent foreign policy. It raises doubts about the Indian government's capacity to comprehend adequately the international environment where its principles and methods attempt to operate. Analysis of this kind is found in the following essay, written shortly after the frontier crisis of 1962. Werner Levi is Professor of Political Science at the University of Hawaii and the author of several works on Indian and Asian politics. He suggests that nonalignment is a strategy that has obtained benefits for India; but the successes came from its use in a promising distribution of power and from certain political skills, not from any inherent correctness of nonalignment as a theory. Professor Levi believes that India has not realized why nonalignment was productive; therefore, the policy has led to confusion and self-deception. This selection implies that India's conventional nonalignment will not survive unless its premises are revised.

THERE is no reason for anyone in the free world to revel in the failure of neutralism to protect India's integrity. But it is a propitious moment for taking stock of its achievements and possibilities, because even in the face of defeat, the policy lingers on in India and retains a following elsewhere. In surveying the contributions neu-

Werner Levi, "Necrology on Indian Neutralism," *Eastern World*, 17 (February 1963), 9–11. Reprinted by permission.

tralism presumably made to the success of
Indian foreign policy, an impressive record
emerges. India has gained prestige, status,
and influence in world councils. She has
attracted support and loyalty from nations
in Asia and Africa. She has received aid
from both camps in the Cold War. For
some time, she remained outside the violent
clashes between nations near her frontiers.
She was enabled to devote her meager resources to internal developments. It provided considerable psychological satisfac-
tions to Indian nationalists. It gave them a
feeling of national importance and the final
proof that independence had truly been
won. It allowed Indian statesmen much lee-
way to decide foreign policy questions according to their own light. But it also gave
many Indian leaders such a sense of achievement and relaxation that they lacked a sense
of urgency about the solution of India's
many problems. Too much of India's planning and development activity proceeded
beyond the people's understanding or participation. The leaders failed too often to
involve the masses physically and emotionally in the national construction work. They
did not arouse the enthusiasm for social
action and civic contribution which suddenly appeared in the fall of 1962 as the
first reaction to Chinese aggression. Ironically, the feeling of unity and nationhood,
which Mr. Nehru had tried so hard for so
long to instil by appeal to reason and self-
interest, finally came as the result of that
phenomenon he had condemned so often as
detrimental to peace: opposition to an outside enemy. There was, however, more to
the failure of neutralism than to stir leaders
and people into a concerted national effort.
The attack from China demonstrated its
inability to fulfil its foremost purpose in
creating an "area of peace" for India.

Many reasons can account for this unfortunate result. There were misconceptions
about the potentialities of the present enemy and the character of international relations. There were misreadings of history
and a misunderstanding of the nature of
society. There was, above all, a misinterpretation of the quality of neutralism itself;
hence its misuse. The Indian government
tended to treat neutralism with its related
principles and assumptions as an eternally
valid philosophy or even theory of international relations, applicable to contemporary world politics, when in fact its practical
value was as an expedient and a strategy of
foreign policy. There exist, to be sure, innumerable statements by Indian officials
testifying to their awareness of the true
nature of international relations. There
was, in particular, realisation that a nation
must be prepared to meet violence and even
use it herself when vital interests so demand. But there was, at the same time, a
strange reluctance to apply this knowledge
to the execution of a neutralist policy. In
most cases, when reality and neutralism
seemed to be incompatible, neutralism affected the Indian interpretation of reality.
The vital role of force in international relations, for instance, had some serious flaws
in the Indian conception, which was shaped
by the wish for neutralism and helped in
disguising its weaknesses. Force, in the
Indian view, was something a nation should
hide from view, should never talk about,
and should shun as much as possible as an
evil. It is called for only as a last means of
defence when aggression has taken place.
Up to that point, neutralism applies. This
manipulation of force was, of course, a great
encouragement to a potential aggressor. A
neutralist would deny that the possession
of force can serve as a deterrent. Yet, by
admitting the possibility of aggression and
justifying defence by force, the neutralist is
illogical in denying a nation the right to
threaten force. He thereby takes away from
the existence of force its one redeeming
feature, that the fear of its use might restrain the potential aggressor.

The Indian ambivalence about the nature of neutralism can be traced to a combination of factors. It stems from the desire
to point the way to a better world, if possible by the powerful effect of example,
clashing with the need to realise national
interests through traditional means; from

neutralism producing many beneficial results in some situations, but yielding great disadvantages in others. It remained true, at any rate, that in the minds of many Indian leaders, neutralism had hardened into a theory which shaped their interpretation of India's national interests and the design of India's foreign policy. As a theory of general validity it became independent of the objective conditions to which it was to be applied in the real world. Indeed, it was designed to produce another, a better world; though what this different world would be like or how contemporary man and society could be changed to fit the theory was nowhere spelled out. Perhaps Indian statesmen hoped to achieve the transformation by their frequent criticisms of the behaviour of statesmen and nations — for they were greatly impressed by Gandhi's success in changing Indian society through teaching an example. Yet, through this approach India manœuvered herself into the position of ignoring the context of international politics which would nevertheless determine the reliability of neutralism as a tool. As a consequence, she overlooked the point when the usefulness of neutralism was ended and a switch in strategy was indicated. This deception was strengthened by the early success of neutralism, which Indians ascribed to their "theory," but which in reality was due to a constellation of international circumstances, mainly a balance of power between the two major nations, which India actually condemned. In short, from the Indian standpoint, neutralism was successful for the wrong reasons. If this was realised, it was never admitted, for it would also have meant realisation that the various aspects of the neutralist "theory" could not stand up very well to the realities of international politics.

A foremost aspect is the assumption that international relations take place in a climate of hostility, fear, jealousy, suspicion and mistrust. It creates a sense of insecurity, leading to armaments, alliances, conspiracies which only create conflict and violence. War then comes because it is ex-

pected. "If you lay stress on war coming," Mr. Nehru told his Parliament, "you lose the battle for peace, and war is likely to come because your minds have succumbed to the prospect of war."

Changing the climate, cleansing the atmosphere, creating a psychology compromise were therefore considered the prerequisite of peaceful relations among nations. India's neutralism was meant to contribute its share of the spirit of international politics. Her spokesmen have hammered away at this theme and have often refused to participate in condemnatory resolutions or criticism of other nations as achieving nothing more than an increase in tension and animosity. Quite logically and much to the annoyance of the victims of bellicose talk and action, the more aggressive a nation became, the more India tried to conciliate her. No counteraction, no show of force was approved until actual violence was used. Any preparation for defence was berated if it included the joining of forces by several states, because, the neutralists argued, such measures would only provoke counter-combinations, give force undesirable prominence, enlarge the area of potential war, and create overly strong centers of power. There was some truth in this assertion. But to criticise such measure on principle was to overlook that it was very often the reaction to previous provocation or the consequence of a genuine conflict of interests threatening to deteriorate into violence. The criticism was in line with the theory of neutralism in which somehow conflict and force and violence could be relegated to insignificant places in international relations if only nobody would mention them. Since admittedly they could not be abolished altogether, the diffusion and dispersal of force was considered essential for the preservation of peace. This may be a valid argument as long as force cannot be centrally organised in an international government and provided also that it would be fairly evenly distributed among all the states so that none can use it against another with a prospect of success. What was proposed here then was an ideal balance of power. Yet, when states attempted by alliances and defence pacts to create a possible rather than an ideal balance of power, they were accused of playing the evil power politics game, so despised by the neutralists.

That a man like Nehru, with more influence over his people's behaviour than most statesmen, should talk in such derogatory terms of power is curious. Even more surprising is his assertion that any foreign policy making power its primary consideration would be "supremely foolish." There was here, as in the case of force, a confusion between the real world in which power is an inevitable element, and some peaceful paradise in which coexistence would be instinctive and spontaneous. In actuality, the confusion did not seem to affect India's policy too much as far as the endeavour was concerned to gain influence in international councils; it seemed more often to affect the criteria by which India evaluated the policies of other nations. Nevertheless, the suggestion was made that the evil influence of power in international affairs could be overcome if nations were willing consistently to use negotiation in the solution of their conflicts. But this was taking a narrow view of power, almost in the sense of force exclusively. It ignored that in negotiation between groups in conflict over clashing interests, before compromise is reached, each disputant carefully evaluates the power of the other. The element of power is never eliminated, and cannot be. The most any society can hope to do is to eliminate arbitrary force and violence in the solution of conflict by properly organising them. But the neutralists hope to diminish, if not to eliminate the use of power, force, [and] violence in the international society also by an appeal to rationality and "enlightened" self-interest. If these could prevail, there would be a recognition that compromise and peaceful behaviour are the requirements of national selfishness itself. There are, however, many weaknesses in this argument. Men are not rational only. It is futile to envisage a social organisation based upon a

nature of man different from what it is. There are, furthermore, values which men are not willing to abandon, even at the price of peace. Quite possibly such values are arrived at through sentiments and emotions, but they are not any less valid for that reason, and probably cherished much more deeply. Finally, wars have at times achieved the ends nations sought, which could not have been achieved by any other means. Goa is a case in point, as are other situations in India's foreign affairs. These cases can also be used to demonstrate the doubtful cogency of the neutralist argument that the justice of any nation's cause is relative. As a prominent Indian put it, "invariably in genuine international disputes, both parties to a dispute are likely to have a just cause, the difference being only in degree." Such an assertion is not borne out by historical evidence at all. There is no Indian today willing to admit this is the case of China's aggression, nor will any nation involved in violent conflict ever do so. Only an unconcerned outsider may be able to adopt such a detached view if the facts of the situation justify it. Perhaps for this reason, the neutralists suggest that there is a crying need in the world for disinterested mediators. It is, however, one thing to be a mediator when the parties themselves have decided not to use violence in the solution of their conflict and have asked a third power to arbitrate. It is quite another, and much more difficult thing for a third power to foist itself upon the parties when they have not renounced the use of force. This was the arduous task India had taken on as a neutralist.

There are two major prerequisites for the successful performance of such a role. The first is that the mediating state has standing with the contestants because it is influential for some reason. This means that the state is a mediator not because of its disinterestedness so much as for its power position in the world. The whole endeavour of India's foreign policy since independence has been to obtain just such a position of influence. In as much as her neutralist policy has delayed or ameliorated the use of violence in international relations, it can be ascribed largely to her success in this respect. In short, the favourable results of neutralism have been a function of power. The other major prerequisite, totally ignored or at least not admitted by India, is that the contestants in the dispute are refraining from the use of violence, usually because they believe that their power is approximately even. The functioning of neutralism thus depends upon a balance of power, to which the neutralist state has contributed nothing and which, moreover, it decries as undesirable. One of the illusions of Indian neutralism has been the belief that its success was due to neutralism's inherent qualities when at most India can take credit for the clever exploitation of the situation in which she found herself mostly without her own doing. Political skill, not any theory of international relations, can account for the beneficial consequences of neutralism. Since the Indian conception of neutralism was that of a theory, the conditions which made it successful as an expedient strategic tool of statecraft went unrecognized as such. When a change in these conditions occurred, especially in the form of China's rising strength and aggressiveness, the corollary change in the use of neutralism as a tool did not take place, with detrimental results for India.

One of these conditions is that India must be relevant to those she wants to influence. The political game must be played in such a manner that India in spite of her physical weakness could establish a politically strategic position. This was possible, for instance, in the United Nations and other international organisations as a result of the rise of Asian and African nations to political importance. As long as their sympathy and good will were wanted by the major powers; as long therefore as votes had more than inherent significance, India's leadership among these powers gave her political power in the international society. China, however, was outside the arena of international organizations and her method of asserting leadership was not to accumu-

late voting majorities on her side but to impress the nonaligned nations with her strength. As far as China was concerned, therefore, the basis of India's political position was irrelevant. As China played the political game, matching her strength was required. India's weakness, no disadvantage with the major powers, became fatal. It was merely an invitation for China to demonstrate her superiority by a defeat of India.

India should have realised that in the absence of any power to balance that of China in the Himalayas, the neutralist strategy would not work. India was no longer outside the sphere of any nation's imperialistic drive, one of the other conditions for successful neutralism. She thought she was, an unforgivable self-deception after the "liberation" of Tibet, the construction of a road through the northern tip of Ladakh in 1956, the building of strategic roads and air fields along the whole Himalayan border, the threats to the border kingdoms, and the softening of the border peoples by subversion and propaganda. Yet India steadfastly rationalized her conviction. The topography of the frontier region made any attack impossible, it was thought, and China could not afford aggression in any case because she needed her resources for internal developments. China's military adventures were belittled as excusable aberrations from the norm: Korea was a defensive move and Tibet was achieving a proper end with wrong means. Behind these rationalizations lay the deeper conviction that "power politics" was a European legacy unacceptable to any Asian. The nations of Asia were believed constitutionally unable to share in the evils of international politics originating in the West. This, Mr. Nehru once maintained, could not be understood by the Western nations, for they lacked the necessary "subtlety." The violent history of Chinese expansionism from Confucius onward; the bloody foundation of the Mongol empire; the long tradition of Japanese imperialism; the centuries-old factional strife and struggles and utter cruelties of the Himalayan peoples could never disabuse the Indian neutralists of the prejudice that violence and expansionism are phenomena of Western societies, rather than human weaknesses.

When none of the usual rationalizations seemed to excuse China's attack on India, Mr. Nehru was utterly surprised. He just did not think they would do such a thing, he confessed. He promised an investigation of the reasons for India's weakness and fired Mr. Menon as defence minister. Yet his warm praise of the Soviet Union for promising continued military aid and his cool thank-yous to the United States, Britain, Canada, and Australia which delivered the aid, may have showed that he was still hankering after a neutralist policy. It obviously was an unacceptable argument to him that the weakness of India began probably in the minds of men who did not realize that neutralism had rendered its maximum service to India and that changing conditions in the world made a change in political strategy mandatory. This is all the more difficult to understand as India herself had been flouting many facets of neutralism, as in the cases of Goa, Hyderabad and Kashmir. By not applying it when India's national interests were involved, she herself had brought the evidence that it was not based on eternally and generally valid principles. Perhaps some vague recognition that neutralism may under certain circumstances be impractical, and an awareness of India's inability to live up to the moral principles she applied to others as she became gradually more involved in world politics, led Mr. Nehru to diminish his admonitions to the world for more morality in international affairs. If there was such a realization, it never went far enough to produce a basic change in the strategy of India's foreign policy.

There can be no disagreement with the neutralist position that a change in methods is needed if peace is to be preserved. But there can be argument about what the new methods ought to be and, especially, how they can be substituted. It is fine to advocate moral principles and better methods of human relations which promise an improvement of the international society. But to try to apply them or, especially, to expect other nations to try them and to hope for immediate usefulness, when they have no relation to the prevailing system, can be and has now proved to be fatal. The traditional methods are an integral part of the system in which they function. They fit into an environment, no part of which can easily be changed radically or abruptly. Mr. Nehru himself has on many occasions regretted the difficulty of social change, though he did not draw the full consequences from his knowledge for his foreign policy. Moral principles and methods of social relations have functions to perform relative to their society. When the dichotomy between them and the habits of the society become too great, the disfunctional principles and methods will give way — in the case of India they did so at a high price. By applying principles and methods which were premature in the international society, India has not rendered any service to that improvement of the international society which she rightly points to as the great need of mankind. Had she more modestly treated neutralism as a strategy, she might have anticipated China's aggressive intentions and prepared for them. China, always cautious, might not have attacked India any more than she has so far any other nation on her borders which is protected by an alliance. Perhaps it is too much to expect India to adhere to all the aspects of neutralism in the face of aggression and prove her case by becoming a martyr for her cause — and it would certainly not be in the interest of the free world that she did so. But to admit belatedly, under attack, the invalidity of many assumptions and principles of neutralism and to make an attempt to catch up to where the other "evil" nations have always been, namely armed to the teeth and allied for greater strength, lays her open to the criticism of shortsightedness and naivety in failing to provide for India's security and survival. Neutralism then turns out to be not a major contribution to a more peaceful world or even only a peaceful India, but tool of statecraft that is risky and was mishandled. Hopefully, Indians and other neutralist nations may learn that lesson. Hopefully also, the shock suffered by the Indian people may produce a national effort with beneficial results lasting far beyond the present occasion.

Illusions of the Nehru Bequest

MICHAEL EDWARDES

A British authority on modern Indian history, Michael Edwardes is the author of *Asia in the European Age* and *The Last Years of British India*. In this selection, he interprets the problems of India's foreign policy inherited by Lal Bahadur Shastri's government and considers its efforts to manage issues during the first few months after Nehru's death in May, 1964. According to his analysis, Indian nonalignment has no effective policies to deal with China, national defense needs, the great powers, or the underdeveloped community. The basic fault is that Nehru's bequest is unsound. In addition, India's nuclear potential is considered. Edwardes concludes on a pessimistic view of India's post-Nehru scene.

IN a maiden speech in the lower house of the Indian Parliament in August 1963, that maverick of Indian politics, Dr. Rammanohar Lohia, produced a pungent definition of India's foreign policy. "One minister of this government," he claimed, "clings to the United States, another to Russia, and the magician tries to hold the balance by his charm. They call this 'non-alignment'." It was not a bad definition of India's foreign policy in the twilight of the age of Nehru and it is not without pertinence today, when the magician is dead and his apprentice, Lal Bahadur Shastri, is trying desperately to make some of the old spells work once again.

But the quality of spells, like foreign policies and gourmet dishes, depends very much upon the availability of the essential ingredients. From India's point of view, some of the most important have disappeared altogether since 1962. In spite of this, there still seems to remain among Nehru's successors a touching, and perhaps naïve, faith in the legacy of the master. Mr. Shastri and his ministers repeat the incantatory word "non-alignment" with increasing frequency as they come to recognise the complexity of India's foreign relations. In his first public speech as Prime Minister last June, Mr. Shastri affirmed that "non-alignment will continue to be the fundamental basis of our approach to world problems and our relations with other countries." When he arrived in London in December 1964 for talks with the British Prime Minister, he went even further and reiterated that there would be "no deviation" from the lines of policy laid down by Mr. Nehru. This would be all very well if these lines had any clear definition, which they have not, or if "non-alignment" meant something more than just the absence of formal treaties of alliance between India and other countries.

"Non-alignment" is no longer the dirty

From Michael Edwardes, "Illusion and Reality in India's Foreign Policy," *International Affairs*, 41 (January 1965), 48–58. Reprinted by permission.

word it was in the time of John Foster Dulles, but its rise to respectability has made it no more meaningful of definition. This is partly the fault of its creator, who obscured it with the diffuse rhetoric so characteristic of his later years, but it is mainly attributable to the legion of commentators, both journalistic and academic, who have sought to erect a whole ideological system around its slender core. The original premises upon which "non-alignment" was founded, however, were sensible and precise and — for the very reason that they no longer exist — it is worth clearing away some of the débris which has been allowed to obscure them. Furthermore, it is difficult to grasp the nature of India's present predicament and that of her new leaders without some understanding of the real nature of the legacy bequeathed to them by Nehru.

. . . Long before independence was achieved, Nehru had decided that the fundamental task of the government of India was to raise the standard of living of the mass of the people. This meant that as much as possible of the country's revenue had to be earmarked for bringing about economic and social change. At this time, it was not unreasonable to assume that, apart from the sterling balances held in London and a possibility of foreign loans, India would have to finance her own progress. It was therefore essential to cut out as much non-productive expenditure as possible. The most obvious candidate was the defence budget. The problem, however, was not so much to reduce the money spent on the Indian armed forces as to keep the level of expenditure from increasing, and here foreign policy could play an essential part. With this in mind, Nehru evolved what might be called the doctrine of defence by friendship, a basically pragmatic view which also appealed to him on other grounds.

Having got rid of the British, Nehru could not for domestic reasons enter into any close formal alliance with the one-time colonial Power, although by sentiment he remained romantically attached to Britain. He knew that Britain, or at least her political leaders, retained a similar romantic attachment to India. These sentiments could be satisfied if India stayed in the Commonwealth, and there were also certain real advantages for her in doing so. In the case of the United States and the Soviet Union, both had been friendly to India during her struggle against the British and there was certainly no reason to fear that either country would wish to interfere in India's domestic affairs. The enemies — if any did in fact exist — were the old European colonial Powers, but Nehru believed that the process of decolonisation begun by the transfer of power in India would take its course and that Britain's example of withdrawal would be followed by others.

There were, of course, indications that all might not be well — the French returned to Indochina and the Dutch to Indonesia. There were also signs in the world at large that the euphoria of the wartime alliances against the fascist dictatorships had evaporated. "The interest of peace," Nehru said in the same speech of December 1947,

is more important (than short-sighted self-interest) because if war comes everyone suffers, so that in the long-distance view, self-interest may itself demand a policy of co-operation with other nations, goodwill for other nations, as indeed it does demand.

These danger signs, however, did not affect the basic premise of Nehru's foreign policy. The size of the Indian army neither protected nor endangered world peace. But decaying international harmony would demand from India more than just a smile of friendship. Positive involvement in world affairs would be needed. Such a prospect held out an immense appeal for Nehru. Convinced, quite rightly, that external peace was fundamental to India's internal progress, he looked more and more to the manipulation of world events as the field of his activity.

The rest of India's leaders, from ministers in Delhi down to the lowliest Congress member, were happy to leave it to Nehru. Before independence he had been the architect of Congress "foreign policy," the only one of the nationalist leaders who had done any thinking about the problems which would have to be faced in India's external relations when freedom came. After independence, Nehru was encouraged to continue in this role, and, as world affairs became more confused, he tended to turn away from India's growing domestic problems towards wider issues not directly related to Indian self-interest. There is some justification for saying that India did not have a foreign policy, but Nehru did. No other democratic prime minister has ever had such a free hand in the formulation and execution of his country's foreign policy, supported by an organic lack of interest among other political leaders. The consequences of this abdication of responsibility are now becoming obvious.

Although she was subjected to criticism and abuse, India did not suffer for Nehru's single-minded attachment to the cause of impartial friendship and world peace. As the gulf between the Soviet Union and the United States increased, great efforts were made by both countries to persuade Nehru to forsake the path of non-alignment. India received foreign aid from both sides for her economic programmes. Nehru's stand won for her the respect of the newly independent countries of Africa and Asia, gratified that one of themselves could speak on equal terms with the two Great Powers. Unfortunately, Nehru took this respect to mean acceptance of India as leader of the non-aligned nations. He believed that the interests of the former colonial territories were identical, that out of their anti-colonial struggle had emerged a community of suffering which transcended national divisions. This was a major error. Respect for Nehru — the world statesman — remained, but his claim to know what was best for other countries was publicly rejected at the Bandung conference of 1955, at which Communist China assumed the major role. It then became apparent that India had

come to occupy a special place which could not be identified as being either with the "haves" or the "have nots." The mediatory role which Nehru had made so particularly his own was, in fact, leading India into isolation. It is probable that Nehru recognised this, and that his outspoken criticisms of the Anglo-French action against Egypt and his silence over the crushing of the Hungarian revolution by the Soviet Union were an attempt to regain a posture of anti-imperialism already irretrievably lost. The isolation of Nehru's India from what has come to be called the "third world" was, ironically enough, increased by the changing attitude of the United States and the Soviet Union towards "non-alignment." Nehru had consciously claimed for India — and had himself played — a special role in international affairs. Acceptance by the two major "have" Powers now eroded any implied Indian claim to represent the revolutionary mood of the newly emerging nations. In fact, Nehru had created for India an international *persona* which was not congruent with her actual status as an underdeveloped country. This statement is by no means intended to diminish Nehru's very real contributions to world peace — during the Korean and Indo-Chinese wars for example — but only to emphasise that these were personal rather than national achievements and that their very success created grave problems for Nehru's successors.

Coincident with the change in India's relationships with the "third world" a breach was also being made in the doctrine of defence by friendship, which continued to pay off in relations with the Western Powers and the Soviet Union, but which failed in the case of Communist China. Again Nehru had assumed, despite evidence to the contrary, that the very experience of achieving freedom created an indissoluble friendship between those who had gone through the ordeal. He also believed that the problems of India's northern frontiers, which had so much occupied the rulers of British India, were products of the imperial connection and that they had dis-appeared with the last British troops and administrators. In fact, independent India did not even bother to administer the whole of her northern border areas. When it was discovered that China was already in occu-pation of territory in the northwest which India claimed to be legally hers, Nehru's sense of betrayal was so profound that he accepted bellicose advice from army officers and others which could do nothing but lead to military confrontation between India and her far more powerful neighbour. Again, it is possible to see in what followed a ter-rible consequence of the abdication of for-eign policy responsibility by other Indian leaders. With the Chinese invasion of the North-East Frontier Agency in the autumn of 1962, the premises as well as the super-structure of Nehru's foreign policy lay in ruins.

When it became obvious that the Indian army on the north-east frontier was being overwhelmed, appeals for military aid were made to the United States, Britain and the Soviet Union. The first two replied with welcome promptitude. The third was not pressed, because India believed that the Soviet Union was in a position to restrain China's aggressive intentions. Many In-dians, in fact, still believe that it was Rus-sian persuasion that made the Chinese with-draw before they reached the plains of Assam. It is doubtful whether Nehru agreed with this view; the day before the Chinese withdrew he appealed desperately to Britain and the United States for 15 bomber squadrons to attack the advancing Chinese troops. Forunately, his appeal did not have to be answered, for if the answer had been affirmative there is very little doubt that sending the aircraft would have led to the outbreak of a third world war.

In Nehru's appeal, there seems to have been an element of panic and unawareness of the probable consequences, but behind it lay a fundamental misinterpretation of the nature of Chinese intentions. There seems no question that these were strictly limited, and that no invasion of the plains of India

was ever contemplated by the Chinese. . . . The 1962 Indian view of Chinese intentions is still officially held by the government of Mr. Shastri, though, since the explosion of China's nuclear bomb, India's appeal for air support has been transformed into one for a "nuclear umbrella" — a request fraught with even more danger than the original.

Revelation of India's weakness eroded Nehru's personal stature, which had already been somewhat tattered, in Western eyes at least, by the occupation of the Portu-guese Indian possessions in 1961. The sudden enlargement of India's armed forces, and the mushrooming of expenditure on weapons which resulted from the Chinese attack, soon destroyed the practical basis of Nehru's policies. The initiative towards a resolution of the Sino-Indian dispute was taken by a group of "non-aligned" nations. Indian policy itself was — and to an alarm-ing extent still is — in a state of drift. Until his death in May 1964, Nehru produced no new model for India's foreign policy under these changed circumstances. Almost for the first time in the history of independent India, other people — some of them near the top of the political leadership — began rather belatedly to consider for themselves the problems of India's external relations, but any attempt to initiate radical changes in Indian foreign policy was impossible while Nehru remained at the head of the government. And although his death re-moved that obstacle it also reasserted — by a sort of retrospective deification — the canonical standing of his views on foreign policy.

It could hardly have been expected that Nehru's successors should attempt any rad-ical reversal of his policy within a few months of the master's death, but there is little indication that a more empirical atti-tude to foreign policy decisions has been developing. In fact, some of the principal illusions of the Nehru era are still very much in evidence.

One of these illusions concerns the "spe-cial relationship" believed to exist between India and Britain. One might call it an alignment of sentiment reinforced by nostalgia, for it has little or no meaning in terms of military and economic power. Indian leaders are fully aware that Britain is no longer capable of playing a decisive role in world affairs. Nevertheless, the sentiment remains and its positive expression in the political, economic and even social life of India is obvious to any visitor today.

Unfortunately, though Britain should be proud of India's friendship, there are dangerous marginal effects for both countries. Britain's claim to a "special relationship" with the United States is given rather more weight in India than the position actually warrants. Indians, for all their dependence upon America in matters of defence, food imports and financial aid, are still rather distrustful of American policy in Asia. India's present leaders still cherish the illusion that Britain's interests in South Asia are the same as India's, and that the United States recognises Britain's "special role" in the area and respects it to the extent of listening to her opinions. This Indian view has, regrettably, been shared by successive British governments and there are no signs of a more realistic attitude from the new Labour administration, which seems to treasure old nostalgias even more than its predecessors. In fact, it would be more in India's interests if Mr. Shastri were to try to persuade Mr. Wilson that Britain no longer exercises quasi-imperial responsibilities in the Indian Ocean and the Bay of Bengal, and that abandonment of the large, static and fundamentally obsolescent bases of Aden and Singapore would be to the mutual advantage of both Britain and India.[1] The foreign exchange no longer earmarked for east of Suez would give Britain a much healthier balance of payments position, and part of the money saved might be given to India in the form of direct defence aid.

Another residuary illusion, and one of far more consequence than the state of rela-

tions between Britain and India, concerns the position of the Soviet Union. Certainly there is no real basis for the assumption frequently expressed in Indian official circles that, in the case of a *major* conflict between India and China, the Soviet Union would openly and materially support India. At the moment there is not even any real assurance that the new Russian régime will honour the commitments made by Mr. Khrushchev to supply supersonic fighters and other war material to India.[2] It is most unlikely that the Soviet Union will repudiate this arms agreement, but she may deliver so slowly as to make the agreement ineffective. There is a precedent for this technique even during Mr. Khrushchev's period of office, over the question of the production of MIG fighters in India. On the attitude of Mr. Khrushchev's successors only time will tell, but it would be most unwise of India to depend on a consistently pro-Indian line by Soviet leaders. There are too many imponderables, especially at a time when Soviet foreign policies may in fact be going through a radical reappraisal.

The third illusion to which Nehru's successors still seem quite irrationally to cling concerns India's position in the regard of the nations of the "third world." The position had changed even before the Chinese invasion, and Mr. Shastri's lack of success at the Cairo conference [of neutralists] last September should have made it clear that there is very little sympathy for India amongst the so-called non-aligned nations.

The reasons for this lack of sympathy are comparatively straight-forward. To begin with, there was already a gulf between India and the non-aligned nations, and this was reinforced by the proposition that India could no longer be classified as "a newly emerging country." This attitude has been further strengthened by the belief, fostered by the Chinese and by such leaders as

[1] Since the publication of Edwardes' article, the British government has announced its intention to end or reduce its military strength east of Suez. [Editor's note.]

[2] After the above was written, Russia began to deliver aircraft and other materials to India promised before Khrushchev's ouster in 1964. Increased military aid to India came from Russia in 1965. [Editor's note.]

President Sukarno of Indonesia, that the course of Indian freedom was not revolutionary in character, and that Indian nationalists were not genuine anti-colonial fighters but *bourgeois* politicians without interest in the continuing anti-imperialist struggle. . . .

Secondly, though they talk of "positive neutralism" — whatever that may mean — African leaders are only prepared to act together in the United Nations on matters which do not directly affect their own national interests. A "community of negatives" with India — non-nuclear, non-aligned, and so on — has little or no appeal. "Afro-Asian solidarity," though still carrying some propaganda value, must give way to purely nationalistic aims in matters of fundamental concern. It is not "non-alignment" that has triumphed among the newly emerging nations but a prickly, self-righteous and essentially self-centred nationalism. It is hard for these nations to believe that India is not driven by the same impulses as themselves, and they are most unwilling to swallow what they see as exhortations in the style of Nehru, heavy with moral overtones which serve only to disguise national self-interest. Nor has Mr. Shastri any of the magician's compulsive charm. There is a growing feeling amongst the newly emerging nations that he will be unable to play as decisive a role in world affairs as his predecessor. . . .

Aside from the illusions, what now remains of the foreign policy of India's first years of independence? There is firstly the attachment to "non-alignment." Since 1962, many people both inside and outside India have suggested that India should abandon formal non-alignment. There seems no reason why she should. It is said that Hindus believe that everything is illusion but act as if it were not. The same technique can be, and in fact is being, applied to non-alignment. For all practical purposes, India is aligned with the United States by being dependent upon her for defence against any new Chinese aggression — though there is no formal obligation for the United States to go to India's aid. This is the alignment of "who answers first to the cry for help" and is the linchpin of India's attitude towards China. But the absence of any formal treaty allows India to leave a door ajar for the Soviet Union. It gives Indians the satisfaction of thinking that they have had to give up nothing in return for everything. They have maintained their independence and honour by having somebody else underwrite it. Such a judgment may seem harsh but it is incontrovertible.

There is the danger, however, that India's fear of China, and her concern with methods of countering military aggression, may dominate her thinking to the exclusion of less obvious but no less frightening threats to her integrity. When the British ruled India, they were so preoccupied with what they believed to be the Russian menace on the central and north-western borders that they were unprepared for the growth of political opposition inside India, or for the Japanese attack through the back door. Historical parallels are never exact but the situation is not, in essence, dissimilar today. The British thought themselves protected — by the possession of Burma, Malaya and Ceylon, by British influence in Nepal, and naval dominance in the Persian Gulf — from any threat to the other borders of India. This condition no longer exists. These areas are no longer under the control of the Government of India. Furthermore, a threatening frontier moved inwards on both the eastern and western flanks when Pakistan was created. The present alternative to overt Chinese aggression in the north is the subversion of India's neighbours, and creeping aggression is probably a much more real danger in the long run than a massive Chinese invasion. To establish friendly relations with the countries on the marches of India, and possibly to follow this with arrangements for mutual defence, would certainly be a sensible though not necessarily infallible safeguard.

Until recently, India's relations with all these countries were, to say the least, cool. Since Mr. Shastri took office, however, he has adopted a realistic attitude towards India's neighbours which offers some reassurance. The dangerous misunderstanding with Nepal seems to have been settled. The question of Indian immigrants in Ceylon — a sore that has been poisoning relations between the two countries for years — has been agreed, though hardly to India's or the immigrants' advantage. The expulsion of Indians from Burma has been accepted in the interest of future friendly relations. The initiative begun in Nehru's last months to arrive at some settlement of the perennial problem of Indo-Pakistani relations, though weakening, has not been entirely abandoned. If all this can be taken to indicate that India is recognising the parochiality of her interests — and implicitly rejecting Nehru's horizon-searching — then the Indian leaders may well be finding a way out of the thicket of indecision in which they have been confined.

In the imperial past, Britain did not fear Chinese activity on India's northern borders for she knew that it was unnecessary to fight China in the cold wastes of the Himalaya. All that was needed was a show of force on the Chinese mainland. There is no doubt that many Indians have since comforted themselves with the thought that, should India once again seem to be in danger of being overwhelmed by a Chinese invasion, the United States would firstly encourage an attack upon the Chinese mainland by the Nationalists in Formosa, and, secondly, would themselves release nuclear missiles against Chinese cities and other targets. There has, in fact, been considerable pressure upon Mr. Shastri to ask for some such nuclear commitment from the Americans. The explosion of a sophisticated nuclear device by the Chinese last October has increased that pressure as well as creating a new demand that India should organise her own nuclear defence.

So far, Mr. Shastri has resisted both these demands. In the case of the first, any such commitment by the United States — even if that country were disposed to give it — would necessitate a precise definition of the conditions under which the commitment would be effective. There is no doubt that the Americans would insist on the presence in India of an American mission to determine whether these conditions actually existed, and this could only lead to final abandonment of the position of non-alignment. This, in turn, would antagonise the Soviet Union, whom Indians still believe might restrain the Chinese from precipitating a situation which would inevitably lead to nuclear hostilities. Mr. Shastri has therefore put forward a plan, the details of which have not been made public, for some sort of collective guarantee by the present nuclear Powers to the non-nuclear ones.[3] The idea is as ingenious as it is unlikely of realisation, for it would depend entirely upon how far and how openly the Soviet Union is prepared to oppose China. . . .

No doubt Mr. Shastri's plan will receive consideration by the three principal nuclear Powers, if only because it has an immediate — though somewhat blurred — appeal. It is unlikely, however, to receive support from the other "non-aligned" nations, who do not see themselves threatened by the Chinese bomb. But Mr. Shastri cannot really wait, for chauvinistic pressures inside India are growing in strength and he may be forced to make a choice between abandoning non-alignment in return for Western nuclear protection, or producing an independent nuclear weapon of his own.

Mr. Shastri would prefer not to have to make the choice, but he cannot stand aside and do nothing. For the first time in the history of independent India, foreign policy decisions have become subject to strongly nationalistic domestic pressures. No ordinary prime minister could resist a demand couched in terms of national survival. There can be no refuge in the excuse that India cannot afford a bomb of her own. India's defence budget over the next few years will exceed £700m. a year and a small-scale nuclear arms programme would add very little more. Arguments that India cannot afford even the present level of defence spending are undeniably sound, but they are not the kind to satisfy an inflamed public opinion.

[3] Whatever diplomatic soundings India made, by late spring 1967 it had not secured any public guarantee of the kind mentioned here. [Editor's note.]

The possession of nuclear weapons by India would offer more than just a symbolic deterrent to quiet the fears of the Indian public. There is one school of thought which sees, in an Indian bomb, the opportunity to establish a Sino-Indian version of that "balance of terror" which finally led to the thawing of the Cold War between the United States and the Soviet Union. The Chinese leaders, the theorists reason, are old, and their messianic aggressiveness is a product of their limited experience of the outside world as well as a direct consequence of the unique nature of their long struggle for power. As has happened in the Soviet Union, new and more reasonable men will replace them in the course of time. Furthermore, it is argued, with a nuclear deterrent India would not have to give up her political independence and could still reap the advantages of being committed formally neither to the West nor to the Soviet Union.

An extension of this thinking envisages the possibility of re-establishing India's lost international prestige. As the sixth nuclear Power, she could by right demand a seat at the top table. And as the only non-aligned nuclear Power, she would naturally assume the leadership of the other non-aligned nations. India could open her own nuclear umbrella over the countries that lie around her borders. Above all, she could if she wished impose her own settlement on Pakistan.

All these seductive possibilities are being sedulously canvassed amongst Mr. Shastri's enemies. Mr. Shastri has very little to offer instead. He can only claim adherence to "the lines of policy laid down by the late prime minister," even though the premises on which these lines were based no longer exist. There are certainly excuses for his attitude. There is the crippling weight of 17 years of total reliance upon Mr. Nehru in the field of foreign affairs. There is the coincidence of a serious internal food crisis and the trauma induced by the Chinese nuclear explosion. There are also serious differences within the ruling Congress party. In both domestic and international affairs, new situations have arisen and Nehru's book of spells offers no solutions. It is possible that Mr. Shastri is searching for a new policy while in the meantime clinging to the remnants of the old. But a recognition of the importance of India's neighbours, however welcome, and a plan for a nuclear guarantee, however ingenious, do not give much ground for hope that he has already found one. The Sino-Indian borders remain the major problem of Indian foreign policy, and the problem will not be solved — indeed it is only likely to be aggravated — by playing around with some sort of nuclear deterrent, whether it be in the form of an Indian bomb or a guarantee from the major nuclear Powers.

Though, in the unlikely event of renewed and massive Chinese aggression against India, the Western Powers would come to her aid, Mr. Shastri must recognise their unwillingness to allow that premise to form the basis of India's attitude in her dispute with China. The decision to unleash a thermo-nuclear war, with all its terrifying consequences for the world, cannot be allowed to rest with politicians in New Delhi. It is certainly not in India's interests that the assurance of massive protection against aggression should be allowed to stifle the search for a genuine settlement of the border dispute with China. Mr. Shastri cannot rely either upon the "lines laid down by the late prime minister" or upon the hope that something will turn up. The first are largely irrelevant and the second is politically dangerous for Mr. Shastri himself. There is a pressing need for India to cut herself away from the past, to discover and put into effect new initiatives in foreign policy. As yet, there is little indication that Mr. Shastri and his advisers have recognised the urgency of the situation, or the necessity for an immediate and radical reappraisal of India's fundamental interests. That this is so should be a matter for disquiet, not only in India but in London, Washington and Moscow.

A Need for Nuclear Arms

RAJ KRISHNA

This reading argues for an end to India's self-denying policy on nuclear arms so that India may defend herself against the threat of China. Raj Krishna is an economist and a member of the editorial board of *India Quarterly,* published by the Indian Council of World Affairs. He believes that there is only one policy that will offer his nation security and influence. That policy is rooted in military and economic strength rather than ideology or philosophy. However, Krishna insists that he is as interested in world peace as any defender of nonalignment without atomic weapons.

Although his viewpoint is exceptional among the members of India's political elite in and outside of the Indian government, it is an important criticism of both the conventional and the amended justifications of India's independent foreign policy which have always insisted that India must abstain from nuclear armaments and continue to work for their abolition in world politics. Raj Krishna, however, believes that nuclear arms and nonalignment are consistent and desirable for India and international peace.

I N the national debate on defence policy, sparked off by the Chinese bomb explosion [in October, 1964] alternative policies which are feasible in the situation that has arisen must be argued out more clearly than has been done so far, so that the nation may make its final judgment on the issue with full knowledge of the implications of every feasible policy. In this paper I shall attempt to spell out and examine three major alternative policies which are being proposed by different sections of public opinion: *viz.* (i) the present policy, (ii) the policy of alignment and (iii) the acquisition of an "independent deterrent"; and indicate a fourth course that I would myself prefer.

The situation that we face has arisen due to the nature of the present regime in China, and its actual international conduct during the last few years. This regime is currently possessed by an intensely ethnocentric and expansionist nationalism. It has a dogmatic ideology, which adds fuel to its nationalist fire, and gives it a messianic zeal and much strategic and tactical skill. It uses, with great effectiveness, formal diplomacy, underground infiltration and subversion, frontal warfare, guerrilla warfare and all the known techniques of propaganda as complementary instruments of policy. Being a totalitarian regime, it is not restrained by free public debate or the wishes of the population. And, in spite of its so-called "isolation" from normal, polite diplomacy and international society, it has won for itself enormous respect in the world because it has proved its determination to accumulate and use power and to pursue an independent policy in defiance of all the great Powers of the world.

In its dealings with its neighbours the regime has furnished unmistakable evidence of its hegemonistic designs. So far as we are concerned, it has forcibly occu-

From Raj Krishna, "India and the Bomb," *India Quarterly,* 21 (April–June 1965), 120–137, selections. Reprinted by permission.

pied Tibet, violated our borders at 42 places, and seized nearly 15,000 square miles of our territory.

It possesses the largest land army and militia in the world and the only atomic bomb in Asia.

Confronted with such a regime it should be the axiomatic objective of Indian policy to try to balance its power. India alone can balance the power of Communist China in Asia, and she must do so not only in her own interest but also in the interest of all her neighbours in South Asia whose territorial integrity and political independence and stability are threatened by Chinese policy. There can be little fruitful communication with those who deny the need for balancing the power of China in Asia. For this denial can only be the expression of a compulsive neurosis to be ruled by others.

It is true that, like all good concepts, the concept of a balance of power has been and can be abused. Defensive balancing can be a mere cover for, and may be escalated into, offensive overbalancing. The balancing nation can dominate small allies in the name of the containment of the big enemy. And the measurement of power is always likely to be vague. Nevertheless, the notion of a balance of power has a valid hard core. The unbalanced power of an expansionist nation is a real menace to which a genuinely defensive balancing is the only real answer in the absence of a real internationalisation of all power.

India's frantic effort to increase its military power to about 50 army divisions and 50 air force squadrons, since her reverses in NEFA [North East Frontier Agency] two years ago, is an implicit acknowledgement of the need for a military balance in Asia, even though this need is not admitted explicitly in official statements on Indian foreign policy.

It will, therefore, be assumed here that every alternative policy that may be proposed for India by anybody must have, and does have, as its central aim, the balancing of Chinese power. The differences between real alternatives available to India today are differences only in regard to the means to be adopted for realising this aim.

The present policy of the Government of India is one alternative which must be considered. The main planks of this policy, as elaborated in recent official statements, may be summarised as follows.

1. We shall remain non-aligned.
2. We shall continue to build up our conventional armed strength as rapidly as our resources permit, and seek the assistance of all the major Powers, the United States, Soviet Union, United Kingdom and France in doing so.
3. (a) We shall organise world opinion, in the United Nations and outside, against the Chinese policy and try to isolate China.
   (b) We shall not lobby any more for the seating of Communist China in the United Nations, although we still want this in order that her behaviour may be more amenable to the discipline of world opinion.
   (c) We shall try to persuade all the nuclear Powers to guarantee the security of all non-nuclear nations against nuclear blackmail or attack.
4. Although we are capable of developing nuclear devices, we refuse to do so because
   (a) we are dedicated to peace; we are working for universal and general disarmament and our capacity to work for it will diminish if we enter the nuclear arms race;
   (b) we cannot afford nuclear armament; we must concentrate on economic development; and
   (c) we are against the proliferation of nuclear weapons because it increases the risk of war.

Let us examine the first three planks of the present policy to determine whether it is adequate for our security. I will consider the objections to atomic armament in a later section.

This is not the place to discuss non-alignment at length but I would like to recall, from an earlier discussion, some observations on the military aspects of non-alignment which are germane to the present discussion.

Non-alignment has obviously not been an assertion of military celibacy for, in fact, we have used our armed forces in defence of our interests in Kashmir, Goa and the Himalayas. Nor is it a refusal to enter an arms race: we have been and are engaged in a conventional arms race with Pakistan and China. Nor, again, is it a refusal to enter agreements to receive military aid from other nations, for we have in fact entered many such agreements.

A distinction must be made between a *complete military alliance or alignment*, involving full reciprocal commitments in the event of aggression, and *limited military agreements* to transfer military hardware or even certain kinds of aid in the field in contingencies specifically mentioned in the agreements.

In terms of this distinction *the military significance of the policy of non-alignment is simply that it avoids a complete military alliance with any one Power in order to permit limited military agreements with all Powers*. In the present situation, the chief merit of non-alignment is that it facilitates a build-up of our conventional forces with aid from many quarters. Facilitating our armament in this way was not the most important original intention of the policy, but it has now become its most cherished advantage. Credit for this development must be given more to (i) the recent East-West thaw and (ii) the Sino-Russian rift, than to the foresight of our policymakers.

Thus the first plank of our present policy—that we shall continue to remain non-aligned—means only that we like to fuel our armament from many camps. The arrangement is desirable to the extent that it keeps up an adequate flow of *total* assistance. It creates, on the other hand, the problems of revealing our military needs and plans to everybody, co-ordinating advice from many sources, and using equip-

ment designed according to many different standards. But these problems are not insurmountable, if the total assistance is substantially large.

It is important that we view non-alignment mainly as a convenient arrangement supporting our development and armament. We should stop pretending that it has some idealistic halo, if it ever had any. Opposition to colonialism and devotion to peace are not the exclusive concerns of the non-aligned.

We must also admit that every non-alignmentist, without exception, has been taking it for granted, consciously or unconsciously, that the forces of some other Powers will come to India's aid if and when she is threatened by conventional forces far in excess of her own defensive capacity, or by nuclear blackmail or attack. In other words, *non-alignment has always been, in reality, an informal, unstated, unilateral alignment with unnamed Powers*. When the threats to our security are as real as they are, this can by no means be described as an adequate defence policy. And a state of such inarticulate but real dependence on unknown Powers does limit our effective independence.

Concerning non-alignment, then, our conclusion should be that while it does not stand in the way of a defence buildup, it is not by itself adequate to balance the power of China at all levels. If the defence system we need is fully conceived, we can conclude a set of agreements with all Powers which gives us adequate security even within the framework of the present version of non-alignment. . . .

Regarding the third plank of the present policy we must, of course, do what we can to mobilise world opinion against Chinese policy. But we have no reason to be very optimistic about the outcome of our efforts in this direction. We can perhaps get some vague and general resolutions passed in various international gatherings. But it would be folly to believe that these resolutions will suffice to alter the basic Chinese policy—which is the only thing that really matters for our security. Nor will the passing of resolutions alter the facts of power. Nations which subscribe to the resolutions will nevertheless maintain their basic respect for the power of China, and try to come to terms with it in their own separate ways. For in international relations power commands much more respect than mere virtue.

Similar reasoning applies to China's entry into the United Nations. We may not object to her entry. But we cannot be sure whether China is as keen to enter the United Nations as her sponsors assume. For by remaining out she has enjoyed an enormous freedom of action and built up considerable power and prestige for herself. Nor should anyone assume that mere entry in the United Nations will ensure a drastic change in her behaviour. She may only use the United Nations as one more instrument of her national policy as Stalin did.

Much more concrete than the programme of mobilising public opinion or getting China into the United Nations is a recently announced proposal, to persuade the nuclear Powers to guarantee through the United Nations the security of non-nuclear nations against nuclear blackmail or attack. This proposal, too, may be pursued for what it is worth. But as far as one can foresee, the four Western nuclear Powers are not likely to be very enthusiastic about it, as it involves for them the incalculable commitment of plunging into a conflict whenever a non-nuclear country anywhere is blackmailed or attacked. *A joint guarantee means automatic escalation.* . . .

Let us consider next the alternative of alignment with the United States, as proposed by some people.

The alignmentists assume that America is prepared to make *any* commitment for our defence, if only we indicate our willingness to enter into an alliance with her. But no one seems to have taken the trouble to find out exactly what the Americans are able and willing to do for us in different contingencies. Before we can even discuss the merits of alignment meaningfully, the

Americans must be sounded at the highest levels as to the nature of their potential commitments for the defence of this country. The unilateral, wishful thinking of some people about America's capacity and willingness to defend us is no policy.

The publicly known facts indicate a rather cheerless situation for these believers in alignment. The simple truth is that presently the Americans have no clear-cut China policy at all. They are bewildered as to how China might be contained. . . .

The present China policy of the United States is indeed nothing more than a series of clumsy improvisations. The reasons for this lack of policy are inherent in the peculiar characteristics of the military situation in Asia. The Conventional Chinese military doctrine is explicitly based on the principle that Americans should be challenged at levels of warfare in which they (the Americans) are relatively weak and not at levels of warfare where they are strong. The Chinese also exploit the fact that it is not easy for the Americans to raise the level of warfare in Asia by their own choice. Moreover, by generating tensions on soft frontiers over a vast area, the Chinese can present Americans with the grim necessity of deploying forces on many fronts.

The course of events in South Vietnam has demonstrated the effectiveness of the Chinese strategy. So long as the Chinese concentrate on infantry warfare and guerilla warfare, it is always possible for them to get the defenders into a long-drawn battle of attrition. The alternative to getting caught in such a bog is full-scale war against regimes supported by China or China itself starting with the bombardment of bases, sanctuaries and supply lines. But starting full-scale war against the Chinese supported regimes has never been and will never be an easy decision for the United States. For it involves, *inter alia*, commitment of masses of Western infantry against the flood of Asian infantry — a prospect which evokes infinite horror in the Western mind.

Nor is it easy to respond to infantry and

guerilla actions with massive, air bombing of the Chinese mainland when American territory, lives and interests are not directly threatened. It is difficult to visualise Europeans and Americans bombing China just for the sake of a few thousand South Asian lives or a few thousand miles of South Asian territory.

The Chinese on their part will be realistic enough not to resort to naval or air action and thus evoke the naval and air power of the United States in the near future.

So far I have talked of conventional warfare. If we extend the logic of the Chinese conventional military doctrine to the nuclear level, it seems that the Chinese are bound to concentrate in the near future more on the development of atomic artillery weapons and intermediate range delivery rather than a long-range delivery system. This is obviously one reason why they have tested a uranium device rather than a plutonium device. Their capacity to deliver atomic bombs through their Beagles over short ranges can be taken for granted. And they may also try to develop intermediate range missiles. But there is a basic reason why they may not try to have long-range delivery capability in the short run. The reason is that the limitations which now apply to a United States response to infantry action will apply *mutatis mutandis* to a United States response to atomic artillery action. While any delivery of atomic weapons from aircraft or missiles may evoke a corresponding United States response, the use of tactical atomic weapons in field warfare against a third country may present the United States with the usual dilemma: full escalation or partial acquiescence in Chinese advances.

The upshot of these considerations is that the naval, air and nuclear power of America is by itself no answer to subversion or guerila warfare, no answer to an infantry push by the Chinese, no answer to a limited use of tactical atomic weapons by the Chinese artillery, no answer to scareraids (without bombing), and no answers to blackmail or demoralisation of China's neighbours by the mere threat that the Chinese *can* deliver atomic devices over short distances. But these precisely are the contingencies which the Chinese are likely to create in the immediate and intermediate future. They will not create contingencies in which the United States power is a relevant deterrent, namely, naval action, air action or nuclear action.

The Chinese will resort to such action only in the very long run if and when they are able to deliver nuclear weapons in the very heart of the United States. The situation, thus, is that while the United States has its massive naval and nuclear air power superiority, the Chinese will not give them the occasion to use it, and when the Chinese are able to use their naval, air and nuclear power, the Americans will be unable to use theirs for the protection of any one else.

The conclusion of this reasoning is that the faith of the alignmentists in the capacity of America to defend us in all contingencies is dangerously superficial. In fact, on the basis of their present thinking, the Americans can do little more for us than to give us hardware for fighting the mass of Chinese infantry with our own infantry, if we have the will to fight. This is what they are already doing. And no *alliance* is necessary to persuade them to continue to do so.

Some persons have recently engaged in loose talk about India having an independent deterrent. It is loose talk because it is not based on any conception of the total defence system now required for the country. The possession of atomic weapons makes sense only as a part of a total defence system, and only if it is shown that there will be real and serious gaps in our apparatus of defence which mere alignment cannot fill.

If an independent deterrent means having a totally independent nuclear capability — strategic as well as tactical — that is, having a stockpile, long-range, supersonic bombers, IRBM's, ICBM's, interceptor and second-strike capacity, naval power, etc., obviously such self-sufficiency is absolutely beyond our capacity.

But on the other hand, we have seen earlier that total dependence on the West, including Russia, will be hopelessly insufficient: it will leave dangerous gaps in our defence against many real contingencies which the Chinese *are* likely to create.

The only real choice, therefore, is that the West, including Russia, provides strategic, long-range cover which it alone can do, and we provide tactical, short-range capability which we can and must have to match similar capability on the Chinese side. The NATO Powers and Russia cannot fail to see this once they realise that they cannot and should not try to do everything for everybody. They must carry the burden of strategic nuclear deterrence, and strategic naval and air deterrence. But the burden of deterrence on land, the burden of defence against tactical and short-range atomic warfare on land and in the air must be regionalised as soon as possible.

Such a *division of labour in deterrence* is what we must work on and persuade the West as well as Russia to accept and implement. It is in our interest as well as in theirs. It will complete the structure of defence in Asia without placing an excessive burden on them or on us and without linking total escalation with every limited engagement. What is required for this purpose is not full alignment with anybody but the negotiation of a series of limited agreements for getting aid of specified kinds from Russia and the West.

In the field of conventional armaments we already have such agreements. But now it is necessary that these agreements must include technical help to enable us to acquire some independent nuclear capability (i) to match Chinese tactical atomic weapons and (ii) to have a small stockpile and an aircraft delivery system. Such limited capability will establish a regional diplomatic and tactical balance. It will insure us against blackmail, and give us a genuine right to participate in all the deliberations of the nuclear Powers affecting our security.

Non-alignmentists, as well as alignmentists, who say that we should not try to have *any* atomic capability seem to be asking not only for strategic abstention but also for tactical abstention; not only for short-run dependence on the West but also for long-run dependence. I am, on the other hand, suggesting that while we may practise atomic strategic abstention even in the long run, we should not practise tactical abstention.

The case for the kind of optimum defence policy outlined above rests not only on the military inadequacy of the three major alternatives, but also on a certain view of the long-run role of India in the present-day world.

World War II was followed by the emergence of two major Power blocs engaged in an ideological and diplomatic cold war and in an arms race. By 1958, however, the arms race itself had produced a balance of terror, which permitted no super-power to move beyond its zone of control without risking a nuclear holocaust involving the destruction of its own population and wealth. This balance of nuclear terror produced a thaw in the Western cold war. But a consequence of the thaw has been the weakening of each of the two alliances and a reaffirmation of national identities, national interests and the will to expand national influence, on the part of individual members of each alliance — most spectacularly by France and China. *The apparently bi-polar world of the immediate postwar period has now irreversibly become a multi-polar world.*

Side by side, decolonisation has been proceeding ahead. Today there are about 116 independent nations and a few more will emerge as the remaining pockets of colonialism are eliminated during the next few years. Thus the outlook is that we shall soon have in the world about 125 independent nations including the Big Five Powers, struggling to integrate, industrialise, modernise and project some influence abroad. It is inevitable that they will divide and form groups on the basis of common interests, cultural, economic and/or military. Each grouping is likely to have a nucleus nation and a number of cytoplasmic nations.

In this context, the question facing India is whether she intends to be (i) a nucleus nation, (ii) a cytoplasm in a grouping led by another nucleus nation or (iii) an isolated, non-descript nation. In view of her size, population, geographical position, economic potential, cultural heritage and intellectual capacity, the only conceivable normal objective for her development is that she should be striving to be a nucleus nation, radiating her peaceful and creative influence over a grouping of friendly nations. It is impossible to imagine this country being a cytoplasm or an isolated nondescript unless it disintegrates.

Indeed, the most precious element in the concept of non-alignment has been the instinctive affirmation of India's will to be genuinely independent and a source of influence in her own right. If this is the role that India wills to play, it is inevitable that she must strive to possess sufficient defensive military power, including limited nuclear capability, so that her image is not blurred by her vulnerability. *It may sound strange to some, but it is true that limited nuclear armament has now become an inescapable requirement for the preservation of our real independence which constitutes the core of our non-alignment.*

Let me now consider the main objections that have been raised to the policy of our developing some nuclear capability. The most important objection is that heavy expenditure on producing atomic devices will retard the rate of our economic growth.

In order to evaluate this objection it is necessary to review the relevant facts. Thanks to the nuclear electric power programme already in progress, we have a 40 M.W. reactor which was started in 1960 at Trombay. We are going to have a 380 M.W. power plant in operation at Tarapur by 1966 or 1967, another 200 M.W. plant

at Rana Pratap Sagar in Rajasthan a little later, and we are also planning to have a third power plant at Kalapakkam near Mahabalipuram in Madras. Besides, we have a thorium plant and a uranium metal plant (producing small quantities of thorium and uranium of high purity), a fuel element fabrication plant, an experimental accelerator, an atomic minerals division which continuously locates mines and stockpiles atomic materials, an electronics division which makes very sophisticated electronic instruments, and two public enterprises which produce ilmenite, monazite and rare earth compounds. We also have a chemical separation plant for plutonium and are going to have a mill to process uranium ore in Jaduguda. Finally, we have a large band of nuclear scientists working with the Atomic Energy Commission in the fields of nuclear physics, chemistry, electronics, metallurgy and biology.

It is important to note that financial resources for all these facilities have already been allocated. Taken together, these facilities can, with some extra expenditure, be used to turn out about a hundred plutonium devices per year.

But there are two or three additional requirements for an adequate atomic programme. First, we need a gaseous diffusion plant to produce high purity uranium. The reason is that the cost of manufacture and delivery per unit of TNT is much greater in the case of plutonium devices than in the case of uranium devices; further, the latter alone are eventually capable of adaptation for the artillery. The capital cost of a gaseous diffusion plant is known to be about Rs. 400 to 500 crores.[1] If it is assumed that the outlay will be spread over four or five years, the annual capital expenditure on a gaseous diffusion plant is likely to be about Rs. 100 crores. (Once the green signal is given, our scientists might even make it possible to manufacture uranium by the centrifuge method or

[1] One crore is 10 million rupees (Rs.). The Indian rupee was worth 21 cents at this time. The estimated cost here is high. [Editor's note.]

a new method costing less than gaseous diffusion).

Second, it will be necessary to recall all our talented scientists and engineers — particularly physicist-engineers who are scarcer than theoretical physicists — from abroad and give them adequate remuneration, facilities and incentives for defence work in India.

Third, it will be necessary to start a research and development programme to perfect a tactical artillery and an aircraft delivery system. So far as missile delivery capacity is concerned, we may only try to acquire technical knowledge for the present.

An allocation of Rs. 100 crores per year may have to be made for these purposes. Thus, in order to launch a limited atomic armament programme an additional allocation of Rs. 200 crores a year would be necessary in the next few years.

Since the fourth Five Year Plan provides for a public sector expenditure of the order of Rs. 3,200 crores a year, it is unconvincing to argue that Rs. 200 [$425 million] crores cannot be allocated out of or added to this amount for the security of the nation.[2]

Regarding the [supposed] contradiction between defence and development, emphasised by some persons, it is necessary to recognise a few basic truths.

In almost all countries which are now developed, there has been a positive correlation between defence preparations and economic development. It is unfortunately true that phases of very rapid economic growth were associated with the armament (i) of Germany after the Franco-German War (1872) and in the interwar period (1919–39), (ii) of Russia under the Czars in the beginning of this century and later under Stalin, (iii) of Manchuria and Japan in the interwar period and (iv) of

China under Mao. It is a mischievous double-think to admire the high rates of growth in Communist countries which were invariably associated with armament and to raise a guns-versus-butter scare when it is suggested that India make her modest effort to defend herself against real danger. There are some intellectuals for whom the Russian and the Chinese armament, including atomic armament, has been a "progressive" development, while India's defence effort is likely to be fascist. It is high time that such progressivism is recognised as anti-national polemic designed to keep India helpless in the face of Chinese aggression.

An important reason why defence and development can be complementary is that the basic industrial sectors which support a military programme are the very sectors which sustain a modern, civil, industrial economy. . . . The growth of the chemicals and power sectors is also essential. Fortunately, it is precisely these sectors to which most of the non-agricultural capital outlay has been devoted in our Five-year Plans. A limited atomic programme will require only a slightly higher proportion of their output to be channeled to defence uses.

Defence and development are also complementary because any armament programme forces the utilisation of idle and under-utilised capacity throughout the economy. This increases production without corresponding extra investment. Further, the feeling of patriotism generated by a defence programme tends to increase managerial and labour efficiency throughout the economy. . . .

Thus armament accelerates capital formation and the rate of growth.

Moreover, an expansion of defence forces diminishes unemployment directly as well as indirectly. It has been estimated that the total increase in employment due to a defence programme may be more than twice the direct increase in employment in the armed forces.

The adverse effect of armaments reflects itself not in the rate of growth nor in the

[2] To stress agricultural development and to balance India's budget, in May 1967, Finance Minister Mararji Desai, a competitor with Prime Minister Gandhi in the Congress party, announced major cuts in the fourth Five Year Plan. [Editor's note.]

volume of employment but in the composition of final output. A larger proportion of output has to be diverted from civil to defence uses. But this may be a small proportion of the total product in a large country, except in a few sectors. And if the total product itself is growing fast this proportion need not increase very much.

On all these grounds the views circulating in certain quarters about the damaging effects of a small extra allocation for defence on economic development, must be corrected. It is unfortunate, of course, that defence outlay has to be incurred and increased but our fellow citizens must realise that its effect on the rate of growth and total employment is likely to be positive rather than negative. . . . The nation must have the confidence that it can and must intensify its defence as well as development effort simultaneously.

Apart from the question of cost, a number of other questions have been raised about our capacity to develop nuclear arms capability.

1. Do we have space to test our weapons?
2. Can we acquire nuclear capability in the teeth of the United States, British and Canadian[3] objections?

These problems are no doubt real and will have to be solved. But the manner in which they are posed has always seemed to me to be very odd. They are generally raised to raise a cynical laugh about our complete inability to overcome the difficulties that will arise if we undertake an atomic arms programme. The very existence of problems is supposed to be a sufficient reason why we should not do anything which forces us to face them. Sometimes it seems that the mood of many sections of the intelligentsia is so negative that they do not want to face any tough problems because they are convinced, to begin with, that they can solve none of them.

[3] The West, especially Canada, has aided India's atomic energy program under legal restrictions stating that the assistance is for peaceful ends. [Editor's note.]

This is a dangerous situation, and I suggest that we must get over it. The answer to the weakness of the will lies in the will itself. We simply must assert our will to solve our problems, because we cannot afford to be hopeless. Great nations do not avoid problems, they regard them as challenges to be met resolutely.

If we have the will, space for testing can be found. One can think of many places; but the problem requires expert technical examination. It is by no means insoluble. In our vast country we have territories with all kinds of geographical characteristics. And there are many ways of testing atomic devices.

As regards the American, British and the Canadian objections, it is necessary to emphasise, first of all, that no nation can be allowed to dictate our defence or foreign policy in vital matters. It is high time that our basic policy is made by us here in India and not by columnists and Ministers in foreign capitals. The force of objections raised by other nations to our basic policy depends very much on what importance *we* attach to them. If our own determination is strong, we can and will think of a hundred ways to meet these objections. We can persuade our friends to see the necessity of a new balance of power, a new centre of deterrence in Asia, that we only want a rational division of labour between them and ourselves, and that it is in their own interest that until universal disarmament is achieved, China's power is balanced by ours, so that their own massive involvement in any Asian confrontation with her is avoided. We can remind them that they have not been able to stop proliferation so far, and even if India is asked to practise nuclear abstention, there is no guarantee that they will succeed hereafter. Also, there are sources of nuclear knowledge outside Britain, Canada and America. Finally if our basic position is accepted, we might let ourselves be persuaded to make some acceptable adjustment in the details of our agreements. In diplomacy no objections are absolute and final. The raising of objections is merely a prelude to talks resulting in reasonable compromises.

It is often stated that entry into the nuclear arms race will weaken our capacity to work for universal and general disarmament. Now, the necessity of disarmament is absolute; in it lies the only hope of real peace in the world. But it is not at all clear why only nations unable to defend themselves against aggression have any special capacity to accelerate progress towards disarmament. The truth is that the progress of disarmament, today, depends almost entirely on the will of the armed nations and not on the verbal campaigns of the unarmed nations. All the moral and political pressure exercised by the unarmed nations of the world has completely failed so far to prevent or slow down the arms race. So long as an international machinery, capable of deterring aggression impartially and effectively with its own forces, independent of the sovereign, individual nations, does not come into being — and it is certainly not in sight in the near future — individual nations and groupings of friendly nations will continue to bear responsibility for their own security against aggression.

Nearly all countries of the world have been following a two-fold policy: remaining prepared for their defence in the short run and working for disarmament in the long run. It is difficult to see why India should follow a different policy. Like other nations, she has to keep herself prepared to defend herself at many levels in the short run, while working simultaneously for disarmament in the long run. She cannot unilaterally transfer the responsibility for her defence to the whole world in the name of non-alignment.

It is an illusion to suppose that military weakness rather than military power makes a nation more influential in pressing for disarmament. As a matter of fact, virtue is respected only when it is backed by power: power without virtue is disastrous; but virtue without power is helpless. The fate of the merely virtuous is often decided in the assemblies of the powerful without reference to and at the expense of the virtuous.

Therefore, while India must continue to work with the utmost sincerity and dedication for disarmament, it cannot abdicate the responsibility of arming herself and keeping herself armed for her own defence until disarmament is achieved. Our whole tradition before independence, and our whole conduct since independence, is an absolute guarantee that our armed might will be used only for defence. And we will be more, not less, effective in pressing for disarmament if we arm ourselves for our defence than if we are helpless.

Another truth which cannot be overemphasised is that from our point of view, any partial or total disarmament agreement is not worth the paper on which it is written, if and so long as it is not accepted by China. Even if most of the nations of the world agree upon a disarmament programme, it would provide absolutely no security for us and other neighbours of China unless the signatories solemnly declare that any aggression by non-signatories will be collectively resisted by all the signatories. But, as we saw earlier, while we may work for it such a declaration is not likely to be made very soon.

It is wishful [thinking] to believe that China can be persuaded to join a disarmament agreement in the near future. It has been impossible to persuade her in spite of the accumulated military and diplomatic power of all the Great Powers and all the appeals and resolutions of the other nations. Notwithstanding all the sentiment and pressure for disarmament the world over China has continued to build up her conventional forces and started her drive for nuclear armaments on a massive scale. In this situation our policy should be to remain ready to sign any concrete disarmament document, only after China has signed it. This implies, of course, that it was a mistake for us to sign the [1963] Partial Test Ban Treaty. China has refused to accept it and we have an incontrovertible case for withdrawing from its commitments if China is not persuaded to sign it within a short, limited period of time.

As for proliferation, again, it is wrong to believe that the proliferation of nuclear weapons will be prevented, only if India does not acquire nuclear capability. That proliferation no longer depends only on the wishes of the older nuclear Powers has been proved by the entry of France and China in the nuclear club in the teeth of opposition from the old monopolists. Nuclear abstention by India is not going to make any other nation practise such abstention; certainly, not China. But it is China's response that is relevant for us. On the other hand, China's nuclear self-assertion may make many other nations think of acquiring some nuclear capability. Some are already working in that direction on various pretexts. Thus, nuclear abstention by us may only bring about the spectacle of our being encircled on all sides by nuclear nations, mocking at our powerless virtue.

Until we have a really universal disarmament agreement the progress of proliferation is a risk to which we must adjust ourselves. The only short-run choice for us is to try to have some nuclear capability of our own and some guarantees from friendly nations.

The common belief that proliferation increases the risk of war has a grim truth in it but it needs some qualification. The belief is based on the assumption that the Asian and African nations who may possess nuclear power hereafter will be necessarily less responsible than the Euro-American nations who have had nuclear weapons so far. This assumption is very weak. If a nuclear balance can diminish the risk of war in the West because of the West's love for survival, there is no reason why the same instinct should not have a similar effect in other parts of the world.

In this connection, I must point out that while the probability of accidental war increases, the probability of a premeditated war decreases as the number of nuclear nations increases, because the outcome of a nuclear initiative becomes increasingly uncertain, and the risk increasingly prohibitive.

Indeed, the risk of war in Asia is much greater at present when China has a nuclear monopoly in Asia as well as the largest conventional army. This risk will diminish if one or more Asian nations, which possess large conventional forces, also develop some nuclear capability. Then, the Chinese cannot take risks with the hope of some gain which they can take now.

India stands today at the brink of one of the most momentous decisions in her entire history — the decision to develop or not to develop nuclear weapons. The need for this decision has been forced upon her by the behaviour of an absolutely new enemy, creating an unprecedented situation. And yet the essence of the situation facing India is not entirely unprecedented. For India has been repeatedly threatened and invaded, and has generally found herself defenceless. But no nation is doomed to remain imprisoned in its history for all time. It can, if it so wills, break out of its bondage to the past. India is breaking out of her past in many fields. Today, she is a more unified nation than ever before — unified by modern transport, communication and industry. She has more freedom than ever before. She has more centralised military power than ever before. She is for the first time rapidly transforming herself into a modern industrial economy under a central national plan. She has a federal constitution providing for a strong centre as well as considerable regional autonomy. She has a growing intelligentsia, dedicated to the task of modernising the nation while preserving what is valuable in her heritage. There is no reason why India breaking out of her history in all these respects should not break out of it in respect of her defence capability. If she wills, she can become for the first time an impregnable and invincible nation which will invite no foreign aggressor.

III. NONALIGNMENT DEFENDED AND RESTATED

Domestic and Afro-Asian Requirements

K. P. KARUNAKARAN

In 1959, when frontier disputes between India and China could no longer be confined to diplomatic channels, the Nehru government had to respond to national and international questions raised by critics like J. B. Kripalani about either the theory or the practice of nonalignment. This selection is a defense of the policy from the standpoint of those Indian nationalists who subscribe to the perspective of world affairs found in Nehru's political thought. K. P. Karunakaran is the author of a history of Indian foreign policy and is a member of the faculty of Rajasthan University. He contends that nonalignment must not change, indeed, it cannot change, because it derives from basic sources in the Afro-Asian community. His explanation of nonalignment differs from those who find it in Nehru's preferences or Gandhian ethics, or who say it resembles Swiss neutrality or American isolationism. In Karunakaran's opinion, nonalignment helps to solve domestic problems of the former colonial lands. Abroad, it works for progress against the status quo defended by the West. According to this view, Indian nonalignment is governed by social and political forces which the Indian government has recognized and led. Determinism underlines this response to critics of nonalignment.

RECENT developments on the Indo-Chinese border have provoked many in India to demand a revision of some aspects of our foreign policy, particularly with reference to non-alignment in the cold war. A few commentators in western countries have already gone to the extent of saying that India has given up her "former" policy of non-alignment.

For instance, following Nehru's statement on India's determination to defend her territorial integrity and that of the border States, a prominent British newspaper published an article entitled "India's Neutralism on the Wane." Another gave "India Will Fight With China" as the title for a news item. In the opinion of a commentator, the meeting between Pakistan's Ayub Khan and India's Nehru [in 1960] was the result of a sense of unity between the two countries imposed upon them by an aggressive China.

All these comments and reports are entirely misleading because the reality is that whatever the nature of events on the Himalayan border, India has not moved one inch from her policy of non-alignment in the cold war. This policy, which is mistakenly characterised as a neutral policy by the West, arises from some basic factors, and unless these basic factors are removed there can not be a shift in India's foreign policy.

Those who perceive such a shift in the

From K. P. Karunakaran, "Nonalignment," *Seminar*, no. 19 (March 1961), pp. 13–16, selections. Reprinted by permission.

present developments will soon be disappointed when another set of developments focus attention upon those very aspects of India's foreign policy which emphasise the policy of non-alignment in military alliances and the cold war.

... In the first place, it must be remembered that non-alignment has nothing in common with the policy of neutrality pursued by a country like Switzerland which enables her to remain out of European conflicts.

India takes a keen and active interest in the international developments of her region. Her people are also conscious of the fact that, unlike the case of Switzerland, her policy of non-participation in some of the major conflicts of the world are far from guaranteed by other powers. In fact some of the powers are interested, or at least were interested, in securing her as their ally.

It is true that in these conflicts, most of which are connected with the cold war, India does not take sides. This does not, however, mean that she is passively neutral towards all. There were occasions, such as Korea, when she took some initiative to end a dispute or, as in Indo-China, when she tried to help towards the smooth working of an agreed settlement.

There are other major differences also. Some of these will become clear once we realise that non-alignment is not the policy of a single country, but that of many countries of Asia and Africa. For instance Ghana, Egypt, Iraq, Ceylon, Burma and Indonesia support non-alignment just as much as we do. It is also interesting to recall that very often the governments of these countries have not only declined to be a party to the conflicts between big powers, but have tried to co-operate among themselves and work out a common policy on many vital issues. Instead of speaking of one neutral State their spokesmen speak of a "peace area" which includes many States. There is no parallel to this in Switzerland's policy of neutrality or in the American policy of isolationism at an earlier

period, which is often compared to the Indian policy of non-alignment by scholars and politicians. . . .

Neutrality indicates a passive approach and a desire to get away from the conflicts irrespective of their nature. Switzerland was neutral even in a fight against fascism. There is no reason to believe that this is the attitude of the Indian leaders. Their desire to promote negotiation and conciliation between the western and communist powers arises from their comprehension of the fact that neither communism nor parliamentary democracy or capitalism are forces to be fought to the finish.

The foreign policy of non-alignment pursued by the Indian or any other Asian government does not mean neutrality in any conflict, but a positive policy of disentanglement from the apparent or concealed domination of a western power. One may ask: does this mean going over to the other camp? So far as a non-communist State is concerned this question is irrelevant, because only communists are accepted as full-fledged members of the communist camp.

Let us now turn to the deep-rooted causes underlying this pursuit of a non-alignment foreign policy by India and other Asian and African governments. To attribute it to the philosophy of non-alignment enunciated by Gandhi and the religious teachings of Hinduism and Buddhism is, on the face of it, unrealistic. Apart from the fact that the Indian Government itself has used force in Kashmir and Hyderabad, and when dealing with many internal tensions, thus refuting any allegiance to a doctrine of non-violence, this explanation falls to the ground when applied to the governments of the U.A.R., Iraq and Indonesia, which also pursue a foreign policy of non-alignment.

The sources of such a policy have to be sought in the history of Asian nationalism and in the present problems which face these young governments.

Asian nationalism, unlike its European counterpart, is the product of three forces which sometimes fused, sometimes followed parallel lines and which occasionally came into conflict with one another. These forces were the fight against the foreigner, the fight against feudalism and the demand for social and economic reconstruction. In view of the fusion of these forces, liberalism, which was the ideology of European capitalism, was never fully accepted in India. It was welcomed in Asia as an advance over feudalism, but not as an advance over socialism.

The fact that some leaders of Asia have accepted parliamentary institutions does not make a basic difference, because in their countries there is no mature bourgeoisie which is capable of defending capitalism together with liberalism and parliamentary democracy. Against the onslaught of socialist doctrines, capitalism is on the defensive in Asia.

The nature, class composition and character of the national movements and their traditions, and the political ideas to which the leadership of the Asian countries owe allegiance, indicate that they can maintain stability in their political systems only through a synthesis of the economic doctrines of socialism and the political doctrines of democracy. This, in its turn, means that these Asian leaders can not take sides in a cold war based, among other things, on an ideological struggle between the exponents of parliamentary democracy and socialism.

From the traditions of the national movements, let us now proceed to the problems of national reconstruction which face the governments of the free countries of Asia. Broadly speaking, these problems are: (1) the establishment of a modern State structure with a strong central government, (2) the promotion of a political unity and stability which can arise only from national solidarity, (3) the liquidation of the vestiges of foreign domination and the complete assertion of national sovereignty and (4) the implementation of a programme to promote social equality and economic development. . . .

In the countries of Asia the problem con-cerning the liquidation of the vestiges of foreign domination and the complete assertion of national sovereignty appears in various forms. Egypt, in the postwar era, was concerned with the nationalisation of the Suez Canal while Iran was interested in nationalising the Anglo-Iranian Oil Company. For a long time the Burmese Government was disturbed by the presence of Chinese Kuomintang forces within its borders, and the Indonesians by many of their rebels, who were helped by foreigners.

Even as late as 1958 the United States Army openly entered the Lebanese political scene, while three years ago Syria was successful in resisting external pressure only by a merger with Egypt, a decision which otherwise many Syrians would not have welcomed.

To safeguard its independence an Asian government has not only to resist open interference by western powers, but also to avoid participation in the United States Government's world policy. The ultimate objective of the western powers is to maintain the *status quo* in the international field, as well as in the domestic fields of the Afro-Asian countries which they once dominated, and certainly to prevent its revision in a direction favourable to the communists.

The primary aim of the nationalist movements and governments in Asia is to make an immediate revision of the international order and the internal set-up in their countries. Some countries prefer the communist way, and others the non-communist way; but all are agreed that revision has to be made, and made in favour of progress. This is the fundamental conflict between the western powers and the Afro-Asian States, and its magnitude is no less than that of the conflict between the western powers and the communist States. . . .

This problem of the defence and extension of freedom for Asian countries is linked up with one of the major problems they have to face — the problem of the establishment of a modern State structure with a strong central government and the promotion of political unity. India and

Ceylon were fortunate in this respect in that the two countries did possess strong central governments and other features of a modern State structure such as the army, civil service and legislature, all of which owe impersonal allegiance to the State.

The experience of some of their neighbours shows that the cracks created in this structure may have very many unfortunate repercussions in the political field. In the modern world it will be impossible to insulate a nation completely against foreign influence. But foreign interference of a gigantic character in such a powerful sector as the army can be reduced to the minimum by a government's refusal to join military pacts dominated by one of the Great Powers.

The most striking case of the major elements in the political life of a country moving towards one direction and the army, with doubtful civilian support, moving towards another, is the Congo.

The damage done to the country by open, organised outside interference is spotlighted in the Congo because it happened so soon after the achievement of her nominal independence. But similar dangers, in a subtle form, exist in other countries which were freed a few years ago, but which are still militarily weak and politically unstable.

Under these circumstances an unwise foreign policy jeopardises not only the administrative apparatus of the country, but its political structure and democratic character. It is not an accident that the gradual entanglement of Pakistan in the cold war, and her military alliances under western auspices, was accompanied by a repudiation of democracy at home. These actions of the Pakistan Government in the international field went against the dominant trends of the country. A government which denies the national aspirations of its people in the international field, is bound to deny them in the domestic sphere also. No country can exercise democratic rights in the domestic field and not in that of foreign policy. . . .

All these developments point to the obvious fact that the struggle to defend the freedom of a country is inter-linked with its government's ability to retain and promote the representative character of its political system. This task can be undertaken only by following a foreign policy of which the main features are acceptable to the vast majority.

In the domestic sphere it also means allowing all parties, including the communists, to function normally. This fact is, to a very great extent, emphasised in countries such as India and Indonesia by the presence of well-organised communist parties. . . .

Participation in the present cold war and military alliances of the West is based on a philosophy opposed to co-existence; co-existence both in the international and domestic fields. A government of a country, which has a large communist party, can successfully oppose co-existence only by destroying the communist party at home. And in a country where the communist party grows under the system of parliamentary democracy, this task can be accomplished only by destroying parliamentary democracy; in other words, by turning fascist. It may seem ironic to a westerner, but it is true that India's refusal to join the western camp, is also a refusal to repudiate parliamentary democracy at home.

Fascism, incidentally, is not a strong potential force in India. The country does not have a continuous history as a compact nation. Her society is multi-religious, multi-linguistic and, to some extent, even multi-racial in character. In such a society the glorification of the past — an important feature of fascist propaganda — can not be stretched too far without creating many difficulties for those who encourage it.

Hindu revivalists of the early twentieth century discovered that their "national heroes" were the traditional enemies of the Muslims, and references to them did not arouse much enthusiasm. In the India of today a fascist type of agitation in the Hindi-speaking area will easily stir up a greater degree of antagonism to itself in the non-Hindi areas than it will generate support in the former.

Apart from the lack of homogeneity of the population, there are other factors which will not easily permit the rise of fascism in India. There are not middle and capitalistic classes which are mature and strong enough to sustain a fascist movement by themselves. The fascist elements in the society are, therefore, inclined to look abroad for support; and in the present international context this support can come only from the United States. This means that, in their attempt to resist the advance of the indigenous progressive forces, the conservative elements in India will be compelled to repudiate the most essential feature of fascism, namely, nationalism. . . .

Whatever may be the provocations of the Chinese, Jawaharlal Nehru can not radically change his foreign policy and join the western power-bloc without giving up his role as the symbol of those [progressive] forces in his country. There is no reason to believe that he will give it up easily; for if he does so, it will be doubtful whether he will thereby strengthen his government's hand against an external enemy. The transfusion of blood which the "body politic" of India will receive from American and other sources will be more than compensated by the bleeding it will create in internal dissensions and the political instability accompanying such a step.

Moreover, the days when the United States was the only source of economic aid to the underdeveloped non-communist countries are over. In the case of the Aswan Dam, Egypt turned towards the Soviet Union for substantial help. India found the Soviet Union to be a more reliable and willing partner than the western powers in the development of her heavy industries. Even the Western hemisphere is no more the sacred preserve of the United States, as is demonstrated by recent developments in Cuba. Some of the international events are so fast moving that one will not be surprised were Pakistan's oil resources to be tapped by Soviet experts with the help of capital from that country.

To obtain economic and other aid from both sides was not one of the cardinal aims of India's foreign policy because we know that she adopted an independent policy even before planning for economic prosperity was envisaged and put into execution. Planning itself was one of the late results of that policy. We should not be surprised to find that even those who have taken sides secure aid from both. The West is aiding Poland and the East moves to help Pakistan.

We, therefore, conclude that there is no reason to abandon the foreign policy of non-alignment which arises from the traditions of our national movement, and which is now in line with national interests seeking solutions to current problems.

The Controversy of Goa

MARGARET W. FISHER

Probably no event in Indian foreign relations has been more con-
troversial among external observers than India's armed take-over in
December 1961 of the Portuguese enclave of Goa in western India.
While many Afro-Asian and Communist analysts praised the seizure, the
bulk of Western opinion objected to what it viewed as a clash between
India's ideals and her behavior. In the selection that follows, Dr.
Margaret W. Fisher, research political scientist in the South Asian Studies
Center of the University of California at Berkeley, reviews many of the
historical, political, and ethical questions raised by the event. Her study
links the issue to domestic Indian politics where Communists had urged
a violent solution, to the Afro-Asian world where India had lost influence,
and to old and new problems with Pakistan and People's China. Impor-
tantly, she considers whether or not India violated Gandhian ideals.
In a creative answer to numerous Western critics, she maintains that
India did not. This interpretation of the Goa episode lends support to
justification of India's action in relation to its declared values and
objectives.

T HE Indian action in Goa last December aroused strong emotions in many
parts of the world. In Western Europe
and the United States the dominant response was one of shock, variously tinged
with distress, perplexity, or resentment, not
always free from malice. A thrill of joy and
pride surged through India. With the exception of Japan, where official comment
was reserved pending further developments
affecting Japanese investments and iron
ore contracts in Goa, and of Pakistan,
where comment was unreservedly bitter,
enthusiasm ran high in most of Asia and
Africa. Peking was slow to react, and more
than a shade perfunctory, stressing Chinese
support for the struggle of African, Asian,
and Latin American peoples against imperialist colonialism. Moscow, on the other
hand, appeared jubilant. Khrushchev tele-
graphed the unanimous acclaim of every
Soviet citizen to "friendly India." President
Leonid I. Brezhnev of the U.S.S.R., who

was touring India at the time, made speech
after speech applauding Indian action. In
his farewell message he urged Indians to ignore Western indignation, as it came "from
those who are accustomed to strangle the
people's striving for independence — from
those who enrich themselves by colonialist
plunder." Indeed, the vehemence with
which a perennially hostile section of the
Western press averred that Nehru had lost
a lofty position of leadership which in fact
this press had never before been inclined
to grant him, was a spectacle which aroused
astonishment and some sarcastic comment
in India. Once the initial bitterness had
subsided, however, Nehru appears to have
become aware that a genuine shock reaction also existed in the West, which could
only be interpreted as high tribute to the
esteem which he had won. It is even possible that he had never before fully realized
the true depth of that esteem. In any case,
the threatened breach between the United

Margaret W. Fisher, "Goa in Wider Perspective," *Asian Survey*, 2 (April 1962), 3–10. Reprinted by
permission.

States and India was rapidly healed, at least at top levels. Cries of "demagogue" and "hypocrite," although ludicrously wide of the mark, have not yet been entirely stilled, however, and doubts and questions continue to find expression.

The principal reason for confusion, in the opinion of this observer, is that the Goa affair is either torn completely from its context and judged as a moral issue in itself, or the context has been too narrowly defined in terms of the Indian general elections. A major difficulty in dealing with contemporary events, of course, is that many pertinent facts must remain undisclosed, and surmises based on incomplete evidence can go hopelessly astray. Nevertheless, the obligation exists to consider key actions in the widest context possible, and particularly in the case of unexpected action, to give careful consideration to the consequences which might have ensued had that action *not* been taken. Another factor making for confusion is that where India is concerned, a special form of double standard is customarily applied which, incidentally, is the exact reverse of that applied to the Soviet Union. Whereas Soviet leaders frequently find it possible to reap substantial rewards merely by withdrawing a threat or by ceasing, if only temporarily, from some objectionable activity, it is India's lot to be judged by rarefied standards, a fate not wholly to be explained by an Indian partiality for moralizing. Prime Minister Nehru is accustomed to accept a high degree of moral responsibility for his line of action, making it easy for outsiders to forget that he does not have the wide-ranging freedom of a Gandhi, or even of a leader of the Opposition, but is above all charged, as he himself has made clear, with a purely national responsibility for the security of his country. Once the Goa action is examined in this context, it is difficult to see how the Indian Prime Minister, faced as he surely was with various unhappy alternatives, could have acted otherwise than he did.

The Indian dispute with Portugal over Goa is not of recent origin. Even before India had achieved independence from Great Britain, she had served notice that independence would not be considered complete until France and Portugal also withdrew from Indian soil. Arrangements with France took time but proved not too difficult, although final French ratification was still pending when the Goa crisis arose last December. Portugal, preening herself on a sense of civilizing mission free of racial bias, took a different line. Had the Portuguese been willing to grant Goa autonomy, a reasonable arrangement with India could undoubtedly have been worked out. Portugal chose instead to amend her Constitution (June 12, 1951), converting overseas possessions into "provinces" in a desperate attempt to retain full sovereign rights. Repeated Indian attempts to open negotiations with Portugal concerning Goa utterly failed, with the result that in June 1953 the Indian Legation at Lisbon was closed. In July 1954, the tiny enclaves of Dadra and Nagar Haveli threw off Portuguese control, and Indian forces successfully barred the way through Indian territory to Portuguese forces which sought to reinstate their authority.

In 1955 the tempo of events quickened sharply. A campaign for the peaceful liberation of Goa was begun by Goan nationalists and carried forward by Indian groups from all the major political parties. The culmination was reached in a mass sortie across Goan borders on August 15, Indian Independence Day. The Portuguese fired on the unarmed demonstrators, killing more than a score and wounding hundreds. The movement quickly got out of hand, and Nehru took steps to end it, although there were many who wished to keep it going. A mass rally in support of the movement was organized in Peking, and further support came from Burma, Ceylon, Indonesia, and the Democratic Republic of Vietnam. Nehru, after unifying the Congress Party behind him, took the matter to Parliament. His position, which he compared to the Monroe Doctrine, was that

Portuguese retention of Goa was a "continuing interference" with the independence of India; that in the interests of national unity and national security — the more so because of Portugal's alliances — India could not put up with this colonial foothold, but that means other than police action or mass demonstrations should be sought. On September 17, 1955, the Parliament, against a noisy but numerically weak Opposition coalition which clamored for more militant action, approved the Indian Government's Goa policy. The Goa border was sealed off in an economic blockade, and all relations with Portugal were severed. . . .

Resentment concerning the Government's Goa policy remained alive. Each annual session of the Congress Party and each session of the Parliament, from this time forward, witnessed an attempt to institute a more militant policy. When Bulganin and Khrushchev visited India in the fall of 1955, Marshal Bulganin on October 28 made a rousing anti-colonial speech in Madras, assuring Indians of Soviet support in the fight for the liberation of Goa. This speech was followed in a matter of days by a similar speech by Khrushchev and a joint communiqué issued from Washington by Secretary of State John Foster Dulles and the Portuguese Foreign Minister, Dr. Paulo Cunha, expressing concern at the atmosphere of hatred and prejudice injected into the situation by the Soviet leaders. The United States, embarrassed by the nature of the dispute between India and a NATO ally, stressed the need for a peaceful solution. Ambassador John Sherman Cooper emphasized at New Delhi the basically anti-colonial position of the United States. Secretary Dulles [through the joint communiqué] took the position that "all the world" regarded Goa as a Portuguese province.

On December 22, 1955, barely a week after being admitted to U.N. membership, Portugal filed an action against India at the International Court of Justice at The Hague, in an attempt to force India to recognize Portuguese sovereign rights over Dadra and Nagar Haveli, including the right of access of Portuguese troops across Indian territory. The Court's judgment was not handed down until April 12, 1960. The Court then held that the 1779 Treaty by which Portugal acquired rights in these enclaves was valid, but was not a grant of sovereignty; that Portugal had acquired a kind of sovereignty by tacit recognition, first by Great Britain and then by India; that Portugal had not acquired right of passage for her armed forces; and that India had not acted contrary to her obligations in keeping Portuguese officials out in July 1954 because of the prevailing high tension in the area. Both India and Portugal claimed to have won a substantial victory, but it was clear that Portugal had for all practical purposes lost Dadra and Nagar Haveli.

The United Nations then became the principal arena for the contest between India and Portugal. An Indian victory occurred on November 11, 1960, when the U.N. Trusteeship Committee adopted an Afro-Asian resolution recommending to the General Assembly that that body should request Portugal to transmit information to the U.N. on the territories under its administration. Salazar, on December 1, responded with an attack on India and a warning that to create a conflict was unwise, as Portugal could neither negotiate nor compromise. On December 14, the U.N. General Assembly took a further step in adopting an Afro-Asian resolution "solemnly proclaiming the necessity of bringing to a speedy and unconditional conclusion, colonialism in all its forms and manifestations." The following day, the General Assembly rejected Portugal's contention that her overseas territories were provinces, formally listed them (Goa included) as "non-self-governing territories," and declared that Portugal had an obligation to send in reports on these territories without further delay. Portugal, however, remained obdurate, and when the movement for freedom in Angola took a terrorist turn early in 1961, attempted to crush it with a brutal fury which resulted on June 9 in a resolution of censure in the Security Council.

On November 13, the Trusteeship Committee adopted a 33-nation resolution (introduced by India) asking the General Assembly to condemn Portugal for refusal to transmit information about overseas territories, and requesting all member States to deny Portugal any help which could be used for the subjugation of the peoples of the non-autonomous territories under Portuguese administration. On December 19, the General Assembly endorsed this resolution. By noon of December 19, local time, Goa and its dependencies had already surrendered, with minimal resistance,[1] to an Indian military thrust which had lasted only some 26 hours. To many leaders at the U.N. and elsewhere who were conscious of the steady progress being made against colonialism, this Indian action seemed not only incomprehensibly out of character, but also unnecessarily precipitate. Before December 19 was over, the Security Council, but for the exercise of a Soviet veto, would have adopted a resolution calling for an immediate cessation of hostilities (which had already virtually ceased), and for the immediate withdrawal of Indian forces to positions prevailing before December 17.

The highly emotional debate in the Security Council on the Goa question was basically expressed in terms of conflicting absolutes. Two guiding principles of the United Nations were taken to be in conflict: the obligation to resolve disputes by peaceful means, and the necessity for bringing colonialism to a speedy and unconditional conclusion. Somewhat paradoxically, the representative of the country [the United States] which had achieved independence through a violent revolution took the stand that whatever the circumstances, there was no excuse for the use of force, whereas the representative of the country [India] which had achieved independence after a uniquely non-violent freedom movement took the stand that if force was required to achieve independence from colonialism, the right to use it could not be questioned.

Had these opposing positions actually been an accurate reflection of the dilemma facing the Indian Government in December 1961, Prime Minister Jawaharlal Nehru and Ambassador Adlai Stevenson would undoubtedly have been on the same side in upholding the need for reliance on peaceful means. Why else, indeed, had Goa been allowed to remain so long in Portuguese possession? For many years the problem of Goa had been reducible to terms very much like these, and Nehru had again and again ruled out the use of force, trying first negotiation, and then the application of pressure through the United Nations. The position of the United States appeared to be very close to that of India concerning the transient nature of colonial empires and the eventual reunion of Goa with India. Why then Nehru's reversal of his often repeated antipathy to the use of violence? Was he indeed flouting his Gandhian heritage?

In the West, at least, where Gandhian tenets are frequently mistaken for a form of extreme pacifism, there was widespread conviction that Nehru had given up Gandhian principles. The shattering of a splendid image brought dismay to many, lessening what little hope remained for a peaceful solution to the world's problems. But the Goa problem, remote as it may seem, was intricately interwoven with the larger problems confronting the world. The terms in which the debate at the United Nations was couched had become at least partially irrelevant, and the manner in which the Goa problem was solved was at the very least not wholly bereft of Gandhian elements.

It is of course far easier to say what "Gandhism" is not, than to define what,

[1] The official Indian figures on the Goa operation showed Portuguese casualties as 17 dead, 38 injured, and one missing and Indian casualties as 22 dead and 53 injured. [Author's note.]

exactly, it is. It is not to be equated with Western pacifism, but is on the contrary active, complex, protean, and endlessly demanding. Perhaps it is fair to say that an essential characteristic of "Gandhism" as practiced by its remarkable originator, was to pitch demands in relative terms, in a manner designed to foster moral growth. Complacency and self-satisfaction were thus forever ruled out for those who submitted to Gandhian discipline. The greater the progress toward perfection, the greater still became the demands. Gandhi thus dreamed of an India brought to a level of morality which would involve complete disarmament, but his concept of non-violence was firmly built upon courage. Such an India, Gandhi well knew, would have to be made up of a citizenry of heroic mold, ready to lay down their lives, if need be, for their India. The Gandhian approach, however, was not to withdraw to the contemplation of perfection, but to take an active part in affairs, and to work in various ways at molding India closer to his dreams, meanwhile taking practical decisions in terms of lesser evils. There was thus no real contradiction in Gandhi's consent to the use of force in driving the invading tribesmen from Kashmir. He might or might not have found an effective means of dealing with the situation in Goa while it was developing, but given the situation as it existed in December, who dares say that he would not have given Nehru's action his endorsement? There was a host of complicating factors present, but at bottom the point is that by December the choice, as had been the case earlier in Kashmir, was no longer between violence and non-violence, but between one sort of armed action and another. . . .

The first public indication that India might resort to armed force in Goa came as early as August 16, 1961, when the Rajya Sabha (Upper House of the Indian Parliament) was debating the Constitutional Amendment for the merger of Dadra and Nagar Haveli with the Indian Union. The Bill was assured of unanimous passage.

The debate took the usual turn of demanding more active steps for the complete integration of Goa. The Government was urged to permit volunteers to cross into Goa, the Communists urging that such volunteers be armed. Nehru ruled out both guerilla activities and unarmed demonstrations, saying that both types of operation would tend to create a situation which could force the Indian Government's hand. To the accompaniment of loud cheers he declared that the time might come when the Indian Army would be sent to Goa, but if so it would be an open effort, and not secret or furtive.

Nehru's statement was headlined in the Indian press, and widely taken as a warning to Portugal that the hour was late. If this was indeed Nehru's intent, the warning was certainly pitched in a low key. He was aware that the Indian public was greatly stirred by events in Angola and recent reports of atrocities in Goa. Portugal's insistence on getting back Dadra and Nagar Haveli was exacerbating an already inflammatory situation. It would seem probable that Nehru had not yet given up hope of a peaceful settlement and that his major intent at this time was to check the growing tendency among his fellow countrymen to take matters into their own hands. . . .

As the months wore on, the pressures upon the Government of India to take action in Goa increased. . . . The character of the United Nations was changing rapidly, as newly liberated African nations swelled its membership. Great Power rivalry was focusing primarily on Africa. India, under dishearteningly difficult conditions, was staunchly committing her own troops in the United Nations' effort to bring about the unification of the Congo. At home, Indian relations with her neighbors were tense. Chinese pressure on the Ladakh border increased, to the accompaniment of threats to make trouble in the North-East Frontier Area if the Indian Government did not stop its military preparations in the Ladakh area. Relations with Pakistan, a

more formidable adversary now with the
latest American fighter planes, became seriously embittered over Kashmir. Pakistan
and China were drawing closer together,
and the Chinese Ambassador to Pakistan
made a cryptic statement which appeared
to hint at support for Pakistan in Kashmir.
India's relations with Nepal were deteriorating, and Indian security was threatened
by Nepal's agreement for the construction
of a road piercing the Himalaya and con-
necting Kathmandu with the new Chinese
highway system in Tibet.

Throughout this period the Goa question was seldom out of the news. As India
prepared for her third general elections, the
issue inevitably became entangled in politics. The Communists, embarrassed by the
Sino-Indian border dispute, were particularly vehement in clamoring for direct
action in Goa, but every party (except
Swatantra) had some sort of Goa plank
in its election manifesto. At the end of
October, the situation was complicated by
reports that insurrectionists had set up a
"provisional government" for Goa adjoin-
ing the Maharashtra border. Who was
behind this? Many different parties were
operating in Goa. There was a strong probability that this new development was
directed mainly against the Indian Government. From early November on, the Communist press in India gave jubilant cover-
age to the exploits of "Goan commandos"
in the border areas, and to plans for a mass
march into Goa, daring the Indian Government to use the army to stop this march. . . .

The compulsion of events had forced the
Indian Government's hand. Troop trains
began moving to the Goa border on December 3. But much more than Goa was at
stake. Nehru knew well the strength of
anti-colonial passions in Africa and Asia.
He had experienced at the Belgrade Conference how these passions could be manipulated for political ends. His success in
diverting the Conference's attention from
purely colonial to more urgent world issues
had brought on his head a furious cam-

paign of abuse from Peking, directed toward
undermining India's leadership among the
Afro-Asian nations. His position that colonialism was dying had, moreover, raised
apprehension in Africa. Various African
leaders visiting India in the fall of 1961
flung searching questions at Nehru. Was
India really interested in African freedom
or only in passing resolutions? No real
doubt existed that India *could* take over
Goa in a matter of hours. Where did
Nehru's responsibility lie? Properly, this
was a United Nations matter, but could
that organization handle an issue in which
NATO interests were so deeply involved
before time ran out? Action in Goa now,
it was urged, could conceivably save Africa
and the world untold horrors.

As late as December 14, Nehru agreed
to postpone action in response to an American initiative for a last-minute effort to persuade Portugal to give autonomy to Goa in
return for a generous view of Portugal's
economic and cultural institutions in Goa.
When this effort failed, the alternatives
were clear. Portuguese authorities, who
had once tried to convince the world that
no breakdown of authority had taken place
within Goa, had already changed this position by December 10 when Radio Goa
stated that some 500 instances of sabotage
had occurred. There was now no longer
any hope of avoiding violence in Goa.
India and India alone was in a position to
find a virtually bloodless solution in Goa
while at the same time directly affecting
the course of events in Angola and, indeed,
what remained of colonial Africa. Under
these varied compulsions, for India to fail
to act could have led to developments
which would not only destroy all chance
for India to exert a moderating influence in
Africa, but also dangerously jeopardize
Indian unity. Moreover, this action served
as a timely demonstration to doubting
neighbors — China, Pakistan, and the Himalayan border states — that India is prepared to move decisively and forcefully
should circumstances warrant.

1962 and the Survival of Nonalignment

CECIL V. CRABB, JR.

After Western countries responded immediately and favorably in 1962 to India's request for military aid to protect the nation against Chinese invaders, a few foreign observers declined to accept the widespread judgment that nonalignment had been discredited. They argued that it had withstood a crucial test and would continue to keep the ideals and objectives it had before the emergency. The following selection is written in this perspective. Professor of Political Science at Vassar College, Cecil V. Crabb, Jr. is the author of *The Elephants and the Grass,* a study of nonalignment. He believes that before the crisis, Western officials and public opinion, especially in the United States, had not recognized that neutralism often serves desirable objectives in world affairs. Crabb summarizes American criticisms of neutralism and interprets the results of the 1962 crisis in international politics. Except for a new appreciation of military power, he emphasizes, Indian nonalignment emerged from the frontier crisis fundamentally unchanged.

O N October 20, 1962, after nearly five years of mounting border tensions between India and Red China, Mao Tse-tung's Himalayan battalions opened a massive military offensive that brought Chinese penetrations far into India's northern provinces. As the Himalayan crisis deepened, American commentators were inclined to interpret events not only as a military debacle for Nehru's government, but as a shattering and far-reaching diplomatic defeat as well. "The most poignant spectacle in today's political world," one observer [Joseph C. Harsch] concluded, "is the Government of India in the wreckage of its whole body of policy and doctrine." An influential journal [*The Christian Science Monitor*] assured its readers that "the Chinese attack on India is bringing non-alignment into question throughout the free world." Prominent citizens like former Presidents Truman and Eisenhower reached the same conclusion. Early in 1963 Eisenhower stated that he was favorably impressed with "how India has changed" diplomatically. In his view, India was "now forgetting non-alignment. . . . It is now a different policy which prevails in that area." Four months later, at a meeting of the Central Treaty Organization (CENTO) in Karachi, American Secretary of State Rusk discussed the Chinese attack upon India. In emphasizing that no nation militarily "aligned" with the West had suffered a comparable attack by Communist forces, Rusk officially expressed the dominant American conclusion: India's foreign policy of non-alignment had *induced* Communist Chinese aggression. The logical inference was that the Himalayan crisis demonstrated the bankruptcy of this policy for India and, *pari passu,* for other nations who espoused this philosophy.

From the inception of the Himalayan conflict, officials and commentators within India, and throughout the neutralist world, offered their assessments of its long-run diplomatic consequences. Spokesmen

From Cecil V. Crabb, Jr., "The Testing of Nonalignment," *Western Political Quarterly*, 17 (September 1964), 517–525, 527–533, 538–540, selections. Reprinted by permission.

for Nehru's government insisted that — in spite of certain other modifications in governmental programs — the policy of non-alignment would continue to guide New Delhi's approach to global issues. Mao Tse-tung's treachery, Prime Minister Nehru confessed, "has shocked us, as it has shocked a large number of countries." He conceded that as a result of Peking's aggression, history "has taken a new turn in Asia and perhaps the world. . . ." Yet early in November, Nehru declared in Parliament that the military assistance received from Western countries "is unconditional and without any strings. It does not, therefore, affect directly our policy of non-alignment which we value. Those countries which have helped us have themselves recognized this and made it clear that they do not expect us to leave that policy."

A few weeks later, Nehru reiterated that India had "followed a policy of non-alignment, and, I believe firmly that this is the right policy." This appraisal was echoed by President Radhakrishnan, who stated on December 19 that in its encounter with Communist China, India's national "principles" had been tested "and found adequate." Among these basic principles, he cited belief in democracy, socialist planning, and a foreign policy of non-alignment between cold war power blocs. Such affirmations of faith in the neutralist credo were vocally endorsed in other non-aligned countries. . . .

This dichotomy — the wide discrepancy between American and neutralist appraisals of the future of non-alignment after the Himalayan crisis — provides the central focus of our analysis. To the American mind, the collapse of India's northern defenses symbolized a more basic diplomatic breakdown, requiring drastic and long overdue modifications in New Delhi's world view. Officials in Nehru's government, on the other hand, together with advocates of non-alignment from west Africa to east Asia, believed that Peking's expansionism in no way vitiated the over-all policy of non-alignment, however much changes might

be made in India's application of it. Indeed, proponents of this philosophy became convinced that the Himalayan episode furnished new and even more compelling reasons for remaining uncommitted to cold war power blocs than formerly. By early 1963, for example, Nehru asserted that events in the Himalayas "enhanced our prestige in the world." This development was attributed in no small measure to India's continued attachment to the neutralist credo.

Prevailing American and neutralist interpretations of the diplomatic consequences of the Himalayan fighting were thus largely antithetical. Whatever else the Sino-Indian crisis had achieved, it had focused attention sharply upon an increasingly grave and recurrent problem in American relations with governments espousing non-alignment, currently representing one-third of the human race. For the predominant response in the United States to the Himalayan conflict demonstrated incontestably that Americans had a most imperfect understanding of the neutralist mentality, of the major connotations of non-alignment as a foreign policy credo, of the forces attracting and holding countries to this doctrine, and above all — of the extent to which the doctrine accorded both with the achievement of neutralist policy goals and with the objectives of the United States in global affairs. In their crudest, least sophisticated manifestations, American appraisals equated non-alignment variously with deliberate or indeliberate appeasement of communism, diplomatic myopia, or sheer opportunism in foreign relations. Even among more knowledgeable American observers, non-alignment was frequently held to derive chiefly from a persistent lack of realism in neutralist capitals in assessing the Communist danger, to the operation of a double standard when neutralists assessed Western and Communist diplomatic behavior, or to a Machiavellian indifference in neutralist circles to crucial global issues, manifested by the tendency of non-aligned states to seek the best of both worlds in the acquisition of Western or Communist economic and military assistance. Secretary of State John Foster Dulles' characterization of neutralism as "an obsolete conception, and, except under very exceptional circumstances . . . an immoral and shortsighted conception" had earlier expressed what was to become a dominant national sentiment.[1]

In addition to a deeply ingrained American predisposition against the idea of non-alignment, three other factors prompted Americans to anticipate sweeping changes in Indian, and more broadly, neutralist policies in the wake of Red China's Himalayan expansionism. Long before the Himalayan imbroglio, American skepticism about non-alignment generally had tended to focus upon the government of India, fountainhead of the postwar neutralist movement. Nehru's India (sometimes in company with Tito's regime in Yugoslavia) had displayed a unique capacity for irritating American sensibilities and arousing American ire. On a succession of incidents and issues — ranging from the Kashmir dispute, to the Korean War, to the creation of an Asian defense system (SEATO), to the Tibetan crisis, to the Goa incident — American opinion was, in greater or lesser degree, unfavorable to India. American reaction to the Belgrade Conference of Non-Aligned States in September 1961 provides a case in point. Official and unofficial sources in the United States did not conceal their chagrin over the Belgrade proceedings — for which they tended to allocate major responsibility to Nehru of India. The prevailing American verdict was that this conclave was a psychological victory for the Communist bloc. Following neutralist failure at Belgrade to condemn Moscow's resumption of nuclear testing or to castigate Soviet "colonialism" as forcefully as Western varieties, reports circulated openly that the Kennedy Administration proposed to re-examine the provision of foreign aid to neutralist states.

[1] Dulles' famous comment on neutralism was in the context of criticism of states like India which objected to collective security pacts that included Asian nations. See Department of State Bulletin, June 18, 1956 for Dulles' speech of June 9 at the Iowa State College. [Editor's note.]

A few weeks later, President Kennedy referred publicly and disparagingly to "so-called neutralists," leaving the unmistakable impression that at least certain (unspecified) varieties of neutralist thought and diplomatic behavior were prejudicial to American diplomatic interests. In the light of such reactions in the United States, an Indian observer reluctantly concluded that (despite some indication to the contrary) in its relations with neutralist countries, the Kennedy Administration sought essentially the same goal as Eisenhower and Dulles: "a closer identification with the West to the point where New Delhi would not be able to escape the entanglements of the cold war." Developments in the interim between the Belgrade Conference and the outbreak of Himalayan fighting late in 1962 indicated clearly that the American attitude toward non-alignment ranged between two predominant reactions: outright hostility and reluctant toleration of the viewpoints and activities of neutralist states in the global arena.

If Americans anticipated sweeping modifications in Indian foreign policy after the Himalayan crisis in part because of their unconcealed desire for such changes, a second influence re-enforced this expectation. This was the initial Indian reaction to Chinese aggression which, along with the responses in other centers of neutralist thought, sustained American hopes. News media in the United States, for example, gave prominent attention to Nehru's confession that India had been "living in an artificial atmosphere of our own creation and we have been shocked out of it. . . ." From the Indian Ambassador in the United States came the opinion that "the effect of the invasion on our external political policies is likely to be . . . profound. The shock of war and the feeling of betrayal . . . has been a traumatic experience which has caused a turmoil in Indian political thought."

. . . A third factor explaining the dichotomy between American and neutralist viewpoints with which we are concerned lay in the failure of American observers to realize that the outbreak of Himalayan warfare late in 1962 did not actually pose a *new* problem to Indian policy-makers. The border crisis with Red China had been accelerating for at least five years; and the relationship between India's policy of non-alignment and rising Sino-Indian tension had been under continual evaluation and re-evaluation for many months. On several occasions in this period, Indian officials had reiterated that mounting difficulties with Red China required no fundamental readjustment in the policy of non-alignment. As a critical "time of testing" for India's policies approached, Nehru asked rhetorically:

Are we to say that when we were safe we waved our flags bravely, but when danger comes our hands shiver, our feet become cold and we want to shelter under somebody's umbrella? Is that how a proud nation behaves? I am surprised at this kind of argument.

To critics who blamed mounting tensions with China upon the policy of non-alignment, Nehru replied late in 1961 that if India had *not* sought peaceful relations with Peking — if instead it had aligned itself diplomatically and militarily with the West — then the anticipated showdown with Peking "would have come in any case, and perhaps sooner and in worse form." We must reserve fuller appraisal of Nehru's meaning for a later stage. Meanwhile, it is sufficient to emphasize that the continued viability of New Delhi's non-alignment policy had been under continuing study throughout the months preceding the Sino-Indian crisis and that Indian officials had discovered no compelling arguments for rejecting that policy as the guiding principle in its approach to problems of the cold war.

After the Chinese attack upon India, the period of traumatic shock — during which India and other nations in the neutralist community seemed on the verge of abandoning their diplomatic credo — proved short-lived. Within a relatively brief time,

neutralist spokesmen from Morocco to Indonesia had left little doubt that they agreed fully with Nehru's remarks, when he told Parliament on February 25, 1963: "If we meet China, we defend the very principles for which we stand and if we give up those principles in meeting China what do we defend? Just a physical patch of territory. . . ." Even while the nation bolstered its long-neglected defenses — in part by relying heavily at first upon Western-supplied arms — Nehru emphasized that India must continue to "adhere to those principles which have guided us whether in our domestic policy or foreign policy. In our foreign policy we shall adhere to friendship with all countries and non-alignment to any military bloc."

. . . Ultimately, more than seventy nations throughout the non-Communist world sent messages of sympathy and support to Nehru's government in its encounter with Chinese expansionism. Some non-aligned states offered to supply arms, troops, and money; many unequivocally endorsed India's border claims; almost all joined in the demand that Mao Tse-tung's government settle its differences with India by negotiation. To a significant extent, this mounting crescendo of support for India could be traced to the growing realization, as the *Daily Nepali* expressed it, that Chinese policy-makers intended "to inflict a severe blow to [the] neutral side and weaken it thereby." Under these conditions, this source believed that "whatever India is doing for her defense (including the acquisition of Western arms) by sticking to her neutrality strengthens to a great extent the cause of neutral nations. . . ." The Prime Minister of Malaya believed that one objective of Chinese aggression was to "prove that India was not so neutral after all and there is no such thing as neutrality in the bigger conflict between communism and democracy." The attempt to humiliate India was thus viewed as a tactic designed to bring other "wavering countries" into "the fold of communism." Arab sources, like the Syrian journal, *Al Monar,* believed that Peking was intent upon "killing the Bandung spirit and non-alignment"; *Al Akhbar* interpreted Mao Tse-tung's thrust into India as a deliberate "blow to the concept of non-alignment. . . ."

The conviction that Mao Tse-tung's regime sought deliberately to discredit and undermine the concept of non-alignment both in Asia and on a global scale, in turn derived from several underlying beliefs about Chinese diplomatic motivations. For many months prior to the Himalayan crisis, Chinese policy-makers had carried on an intensive, increasingly intemperate, propaganda campaign against Nehru's government, a prominent theme of which was that New Delhi's professed non-alignment was a sham and merely a thinly disguised pose to conceal India's growing ties with, and dependence upon, "Western imperialists." Mao Tse-tung's government, said India's Foreign Minister, had repeatedly contended that "our policy of non-alignment is hypocrisy, that we are already aligned to the Western bloc, and this (Himalayan) war . . . is induced by the Western bloc, and we are using it to exploit the poor people of our country."

The extent to which Chinese officials actually believed their own accusations against India is impossible to determine with assurance. Americans — conscious of New Delhi's resistance to participation in a Western-sponsored security pact in Asia and its earlier reluctance to accept American arms-aid — would naturally be tempted to interpret Chinese allegations as sheer fabrications, designed to rationalize Peking's own aggressiveness. However tempting such an explanation might be, it appeared too simple to account satisfactorily for Communist Chinese viewpoints.

Even certain Western observers believed that, as India became stronger economically, at least the *possibility* existed that New Delhi might try to assert its own Himalayan border claims by force, and (if in no other way than morally and diplomatically) it would be supported in this endeavor by the West. Moreover, Chinese policy-makers

could hardly be unmindful of the American tendency to look upon a free and democratic, economically developing India as perhaps the chief bulwark against Communist inroads in Asia or, more broadly, as "the pivotal hope of the developing world." There was the additional fact that (however uncommitted India might be diplomatically and militarily) Nehru's government was in reality still very dependent upon outside countries, chiefly Western countries, economically and financially. In addition, Chinese officials were more fully aware of another fact about India and other leading neutralist nations than many public commentators and even some officials in the United States. A major tenet of Nehru's non-alignment philosophy was that, on the plane of *ideology,* India was totally and unequivocally committed to the side of the free world in its attachment to broad humanitarian goals and in its reliance upon democratic processes for achieving these goals. Or, as an American official expressed it, most neutralist nations were

neutralist only in that they have not joined the mutual security system. . . . they are not neutralist when it comes to deciding in favor of human values of freedom and the dignity of the individual, as espoused by the United States and its friends. . . .

Yet these factors may have been subordinate to another in explaining why opinion in India and in other neutralist circles believed Mao Tse-tung's government sought to discredit and to destroy the concept of non-alignment. Red China's Himalayan venture had to be understood against a background of steadily deteriorating Sino-Soviet relations. . . .

Even before the graphic emergence of neutralism as an influential global force (first highlighted by the Bandung Afro-Asian Conference in 1955), a careful weighing of strategic alternatives, in a global context of contending ideologies and great power animosities, attracted nations in Asia, the Arab world, and Africa to a position of non-alignment. After 1955 these

strategic arguments proved equally compelling in winning adherents to the neutralist cause. The Sino-Indian crisis late in
1962 provided a testing-ground for the
validity of the strategic postulates supporting the doctrine. Ultimately, the vast majority of neutralist governments not only
concluded that the military-defense calculations underlying a non-aligned position
were basically sound; they discovered *new*
strategic arguments tending to make the
case for non-alignment more persuasive
than ever before. Six aspects of the strategic problem confronting neutralist policy
officials after Red China's Himalayan attack accounted for these conclusions.

The first of these involved a transcendent
danger recognized in neutralist, Western,
and Communist capitals alike: the risk that
the Himalayan conflict might escalate into a
regional or global holocaust. Every country
directly or indirectly involved in the dispute
(from all the evidence, including Red
China) sought to confine the Himalayan
fighting to the smallest possible dimensions
and, above all, to avoid a nuclear cold war
confrontation on Indian soil. As a goal
uppermost in the minds of Indian officials
before the outbreak of Himalayan warfare,
this objective was even more paramount
after the crisis. Barely a week after the
Sino-Indian conflict erupted, Nehru declared that India wanted nothing to do with
nuclear weapons in its encounter with Red
China.[2] A few days later, Indian diplomats
in Washington were said to believe that
"India wishes above all to keep the Communist Chinese attack from escalating into
a major war. Hence, India is refusing
Britain's proffers of specialized troops and
is avoiding anything like bombing raids
inside China." This report stated that New
Delhi "also strongly rejects any talk of resort
to nuclear warfare, including the use of
tactical atomic weapons . . . assuming these

should be offered by the United States."
Many of these same objectives applied to
suggestions that Western ground forces be
sent to India or that, as Chinese troops
pushed deeper into Indian soil, a Western
"air umbrella" be thrown over the Indian
subcontinent. The *Times of India* pointed
out that anything more than emergency
arms-aid from the West would "threaten
to destroy the delicate balance of interests
between the Soviet Union and the United
States" that was being achieved as an out-
growth of the Cuban crisis. Consequently,
a "large-scale flow of military aid to India
from the West" might prove far more inimical than beneficial to Indian security.

Deep concern about the danger of military escalation was no less prevalent in
Washington and London; such apprehension re-enforced the tendency of policy-
makers in New Delhi to preserve India's
non-aligned position. Although chagrin
over India's neutralism had colored official
and public American attitudes in the past,
events revealed that the Kennedy Administration was not indifferent to the strategic
implications attending any contemplated
abandonment of non-alignment by Nehru's
government. From the very inception of
the Himalayan crisis, therefore, American
officials stated categorically that *they did
not want* New Delhi to forsake non-alignment, nor was there any official American
encouragement to the government of India
to request a Western security guarantee.
Deeply embroiled themselves in a crisis
with the Soviet Union over Cuba, and increasingly involved in lesser crises in Laos
and South Vietnam, officials in the United
States clearly did not relish the prospect of
a new, and possibly massive, American
military commitment on the Indian subcontinent. . . .

A third strategic consideration was a corollary of the second. It related to the
nature and effectiveness of any proposed
Western (meaning chiefly American) military involvement in the Sino-Indian crisis.
As policy-makers in India and other non-
aligned countries weighed the future of

[2] Units of the United States Seventh Fleet entered
the Bay of Bengal during the 1962 Sino-Indian
crisis. In March 1965 the Department of State
denied reports in India that the units had included
an aircraft carrier with nuclear weapons. [Editor's
note.]

neutralism as a foreign policy principle, they assessed anew a question that had always been pivotal in attracting nations to the neutralist camp. Suppose that India *did* abandon non-alignment in the wake of Peking's aggression and that it took the next logical step of entering a Western-sponsored alliance like SEATO. Would this step actually *enhance* Indian security? After Red China's aggression, as in the past, policy-makers in India and other neutralist nations remained convinced that the strategic disadvantages of such a move significantly outweighed the advantages. From the vantage point solely of military security, New Delhi still believed that India had little to gain and much to lose by such a step.

. . . A fourth security consideration leading neutralist governments to conclude that their strategic well-being would not be served by forsaking non-alignment relates intimately to a point we have already discussed — the progressively more acrimonious Sino-Soviet dispute. On the strategic level, neutralist policy-makers from Africa to the Orient were convinced that the problem of national defense would be made infinitely more difficult if, by abandoning non-alignment, they greatly enhanced Peking's position vis-à-vis Moscow's and correspondingly reduced Soviet influence in restraining Chinese diplomatic "adventurism." Despite its attempt to preserve a position of publicly unobtrusive neutrality in the Sino-Indian quarrel, the Kremlin was known to be acutely embarrassed by Mao's expansionist policies. . . .

Even before the eruption of fighting along the Sino-Indian border, a basic premise of Indian defense and strategic planning was that relations with Communist China would remain hostile for an indefinite period in the future and that tensions would take diverse forms, from continuing ideological and propaganda belligerency to possible renewals of outright warfare. Moreover, officials in New Delhi believed that bolstering India's defenses against the possibility of new Chinese military onslaughts

had to be done at no expense to the nation's ambitious development programs. The success of these projects was viewed by Nehru's government as no less vital to national survival and the preservation of freedom than an expanded military-defense mechanism. From these premises, Indian officials were led to emphasize a fifth aspect of the security problem facing their country: the nation's dependence upon continued (hopefully, expanded) Soviet economic and technical assistance. Uninterrupted Soviet aid was deemed indispensable in enabling India to carry the new defense burden now required, while maintaining internal development programs unimpaired. Britain and the United States had been unstinting in providing emergency military assistance to Nehru's harassed government. Yet, as New Delhi was now required to double its defense budget to a total of $1.8 billion annually, India became more dependent than ever upon outside assistance. For example, the drain on its foreign exchange occasioned by the preparedness measures now demanded was described by one Indian official as potentially disastrous. Even as Indian dependence upon other countries increased, however, there appeared little prospect that the scope of American or other Western economic and technical assistance would be expanded to cover the nation's future requirements. Indeed, by early 1963, Indian commentators called attention to persistent misgivings on Capitol Hill about Nehru's government and to a widespread legislative desire to *reduce* American foreign aid programs. Indians thus anticipated a likely contraction in (or, at any rate, a reluctance to increase) development assistance funds from the United States, at the very time their foreign aid requirements were greater than at any period in the past.

Accordingly, in the midst of the Himalayan conflict, Indian envoys visited the Soviet Union and other friendly countries to secure promises of foreign aid. In Moscow, Soviet pledges were obtained in behalf of India's current Third Plan and promises of Soviet assistance for the forthcoming Fourth Plan. In this venture, Indian officials emphasized to Communist policy-makers in Europe that

non-alignment and peaceful co-existence would continue to be the basic features of India's foreign policy. If India was obtaining military assistance from the West . . . it did not in any way conflict with its policy of non-alignment. . . . For non-alignment did not mean surrender to aggression.

A sixth dimension of the security problem facing India may well have been pivotal in persuading Nehru's government to reassert its attachment to non-alignment in the wake of Red China's Himalayan attack. Unlike other aspects of the security problem, this related not so much to tangible gains like expanded foreign assistance or an enhanced military position: it had to do more with the intangible — but in the Indian view, absolutely vital — realm of national attitudes and public morale in dealing with the omnipresent challenge of Chinese expansionism. For India, as for other societies throughout the neutralist zone, non-alignment in foreign affairs had always been linked intimately with the acquisition and maintenance of national independence. As an Indian commentator emphasized late in 1962, it was an "expression of the will to be free." Abandonment of this principle would tend to isolate India "further still from the emerging nations of Asia and Africa," since a diplomatic position of non-alignment was regarded as a concomitant of genuine independence by a growing circle of nations throughout this region.

As with other arguments tending to support the doctrine of non-alignment, Nehru and members of his government did not believe that the worsening crisis with China altered the necessity for Indians alone to accept primary responsibility for safeguarding national security. . . . This conviction led logically to the corollary that in maintaining the new spirit Peking's attack had engendered throughout India, the doctrine

of non-alignment played a key role. Psychologically, nationalist leaders like Nehru had always relied upon this policy to demonstrate graphically the reality of independence in policy formulation. Now, as in the past, military alignment with the West might tend to foster popular attitudes prejudicial to the spirit of self-sacrifice, the sense of national unity, and the determination to shoulder responsibilities that were required to preserve national integrity. Nehru declared that repudiation of non-alignment might imply to the Indian masses that "somebody will protect us and we need not do it ourselves." For this reason, he told a cheering Parliament that if a policy choice had to be made, his government would prefer high national morale and a strong sense of unity and dedication at home above all the military assistance that might be furnished by countries friendly to India.

Reviewing the arguments for and against the idea of non-alignment, an editorial in the *Indian Express* concluded:

On their side, the West must realize — as to some extent they do — that India must maintain its non-aligned front against the obvious Chinese efforts to damage and destroy it. We do so in the consciousness that we now know at least who our friends are.

That the strategic realities underlying the Indian decision were appreciated by officials in Washington (if not by the American society as a whole) was illustrated when Nehru told a mass rally in India that "the head of one Western country now giving us arms has written me saying he had not wanted India to change its traditional policy of non-alignment." Nehru did not identify this official, but one report noted "the audience believed he meant President Kennedy. One could hear the name of President Kennedy passed from person to person."

. . . Our analysis of the testing of non-alignment suggests several conclusions. These may conveniently be grouped into two broad categories: those directly affecting India and other countries professing non-alignment as a guiding principle of foreign policy, and those particularly relevant for a more realistic and objective American understanding of neutralist viewpoints and policies. In the former category, surely the dominant conclusion is that the doctrine of non-alignment emerged from the fires of the Himalayan conflict basically intact. Policy-makers in New Delhi and other neutralist capitals concluded that, on balance, Red China's attack upon India *strengthened* the case for the neutralist ideology, both by showing the continued validity of existing arguments, and by supplying new arguments in behalf of the concept. As our discussion has emphasized, this verdict stemmed from more than a tendency to perpetuate long-cherished attitudes in foreign affairs, from an absence of "realism" in appraising influences shaping national policy, from the dominance of emotional-psychological factors over rational calculations in arriving at national goals and strategies, or from ideological vested interest. In this period, as formerly, neutralist countries were induced to follow the path of non-alignment between cold war power blocs primarily because, in the view of national officials, this course best achieved internal and external policy objectives.

Admittedly, the doctrine of non-alignment emerged "purified and toughened" from the Himalayan imbroglio. Indian officials conceded readily (and other neutralist officials conceded implicitly) that, in Nehru's words, "there is no non-alignment vis-à-vis China." To that extent, it could correctly be asserted that India's expression and practice of non-alignment had undergone a fundamental change. Yet this change, however widely it might be applauded in the United States, itself posed potentially troublesome issues in American relations with neutralist countries. For it meant that India, in company with almost all other states in the neutralist community, put considerable emphasis upon a distinction that had tended to receive little attention in American policies and viewpoints toward the Communist bloc. This was the divergence between Soviet and Chinese Communist goals and tactics in world affairs. If it could now be said that India was no longer non-aligned in its relations with Red China, this meant that the Sino-Soviet dispute was regarded by Indian policy-makers as well-nigh irreconcilable and permanent. This conclusion stemmed, in turn, from an Indian (and more broadly, neutralist) propensity to emphasize the role of historical, geographical, demographic, strategic, and cultural influences over ideological forces in explaining the diplomatic behavior of powerful Communist states. Neither in the Himalayan crisis, nor earlier, were India and other neutralist countries inclined to regard the Communist bloc as monolithic, or nearly so; nor did they accept the prevalent American assessment that episodes like the Himalayan conflict had their origins primarily in the machinations of international communism. In this respect, the Himalayan encounter between India and Red China could be expected to perpetuate differing neutralist and American appraisals of communism as a global movement and to engender future disagreements deriving from these appraisals. . . .

For Americans, no less than for Indians, the crisis in the Himalayas demanded objective soul-searching and a willingness to reappraise deep-seated national attitudes. The Himalayan experience, for example, clearly revealed that there exist numerous gradations or levels of non-alignment, and that these are variously compatible with the attainment of American diplomatic objectives. Both before and after the Sino-Indian encounter, Nehru's government was determined to remain *militarily* non-aligned, in the sense that it was unwilling to enter a Western-sponsored alliance system. Similarly, Indian officials reiterated their determination to remain *diplomatically* non-aligned; in the months following the outbreak of Himalayan warfare, as before, there was no diminution in India's determination to take diplomatic positions at the UN or elsewhere in the face of opposition by the Western or Communist blocs. *Ideologically,* India's non-alignment was another matter. In whatever degree Indian or American opinion alike often seemed oblivious to the fact, Nehru's government had always been committed to the West ideologically, in the defense of freedom and democratic institutions. Even though Indian officials had said so many times prior to 1962, the Sino-Indian crisis underscored the fact that, as one Indian source put it, "even if we profess to remain neutral and non-aligned, our sympathies will be wholly in favour of the West to which we are deeply beholden."

Progressive Neutralism

V. K. KRISHNA MENON

In late 1962, V. K. Krishna Menon left the Indian cabinet because of Chinese frontier victories; in early 1967, he was defeated for reelection to Parliament as an independent candidate after the Congress party refused to renominate him in his Bombay constituency. Despite these difficulties, the controversial former Defense Minister had influential moments in Indian politics during these years based on his service to Indian nationalism, his close association with Nehru, and his following in the Congress party's left wing. In this selection he answers Indian commentators who had suggested drastic alterations in the ideology and means of nonalignment. Warning against changes that might damage India's welfare, he does not deny these critics' frequent view that national interest is the main test for Indian foreign policy. Krishna Menon affirms self-reliance as a first principle, leading him to demand that India should not purchase food or permit Western involvement in Indian industries. He interprets China as a political rather than a military challenge, and his views on Indian diplomacy toward that country vary from popular Indian attitudes. One of the best publicized Indian leaders of the last two decades, Krishna Menon believes that nonalignment has served certain values and interests in the past and will be productive in the future, if protected from its foes at home and abroad.

THE objectives of foreign policy, as of diplomacy which is the instrument of its implementation, is to strengthen friendships, to neutralise those less friendly and to prevent the combining of enemies. Forging and strengthening of friendships is in the last analysis a matter of mutual interest and the recognition of it. Neutralisation is also in the same category but, perhaps, it is the counsel of reducing prospective foes to lesser evils. This aim compels flexibility in policy, negotiations, compromises and concessions. It also concedes not infrequently to bluff, miscalculation and conflict. These are dangers mainly engendered by opportunism and disregard of the legitimate interest of others.

The foreign policy of India is more often spoken of as "non-alignment" than by any other appellation. The "Five Principles" — *"Pancha Shila"* — is also, though to a lesser extent, spoken of as India's foreign policy.

From V. K. Menon, "Foreign Policy Continuum," *Seminar,* no. 75 (November 1965), pp. 41–50, selections. Reprinted by permission.

Neither of these labels help to explain or truly connote the foreign policy of India or the conduct of it. . . .

The main bases of it are (a) non-alignment, (b) support of the freedom of colonial peoples and (c) opposition to racism. The enunciation of these bases again do not fully explain either the motivations or the content of the policy as a whole or on each occasion. All three of them have, on the face of it, a negative or "agin it" ring by themselves; they do not fully explain the conduct or contribution of India in world affairs.

World peace and co-existence as goals or motivating factors more fully explain a great part of it. It would be somewhat superficial and unhistoric to contend that even these truly explain our motivations.

Ours is a world of nation States. The dream or hope of "One World" does not belie this stubborn fact. Ours is also a world in which strife, war and conflict are inherent in the relations between nations. The foreign policy of India does not exclude the use of force or the threats of it, or the preparedness against these. The avoidance of conflict and policies directed to such an end are not excluded by this fact.

From what I have said above, as well as from the fact of the birth-roots of our independence, it follows that nationalism plays both a key and conclusive role in our motivations and conduct. . . .

Non-alignment is . . . the policy of independence. It reserves and stoutly maintains that India will make its own decisions in her national interests and in conformity with her ideas of what is good in world interests. A policy of alignment with foreign States on the other hand, especially when the partner to the alignment is economically and militarily much weaker perforce places the decision in foreign hands. It is also a policy based on self-reliance and national dignity. . . .

The Five Principles are "self-interest" formulations. They are mutual respect, mutual interests, non-interference in others'

internal affairs and reciprocity. The very idea of "mutuality" is based on self-respect and self-interest. Not only does respect which is not "mutual" become subservience, but it fails to insure the respect for oneself in which mutuality rests. It is a self-interest. Mutual interests require no explanation. It is plain, realistic, down to earth self-respect. Reciprocity which has always been, and even before the enunciation of the Five Principles, integral to our policy is again self-respect and self-interest. When we negotiated Commonwealth relations and discussed the bases on which such relations could rest, "reciprocity" was one of them. We practise it in our relations with South Africa, in tariff policies and in the closeness or otherwise of our relations with countries in the world and in the United Nations.

5781—Heath—Power: Nonalignment . .65

India's foreign policy, again, while seeking (a) no great power status; (b) no leadership of any group of nations, has as a matter of fact resulted in the elevation of India to the status and functional position of one of the great nations of the world. These are consistent with her size, her economic development (comparatively) and her strategic position. . . .

Foreign policy must yield results. What produces adverse results is poor policy. The latter must stand or fall by the results it yields. This is not to be cynical about ideals or the ethical content of policies. It must stand justified by implementations which fulfil the aim of policy. The aim of foreign policy and of the diplomacy which should implement it is the safeguarding of national interests; that is to say, safeguarding territorial, political and economic integrity of the concerned States. Policy must secure the country not only against military aggression but economic penetration and domination and against strategic offensives or intrusions from neighbouring areas or locations.

It is not my purpose to catalogue Indian achievements which at best in international affairs can only be partly India's in any event, but to help to examine the new crisis prescriptions in the light of the record of our policies and their successes. We are too near events perhaps to assess it in sound perspective. India's contribution in world affairs is not easy to be isolated for another reason. Her deliberate approach and technique has been to work quietly, to put forward proposals, along with other States, often to obtain results by amendment to resolutions of opponents and induce them to accept them and to avoid allocation of blames, particularly condemnations.

In regard to Korea, Vietnam, the Congo, Palestine, Cyprus, the Suez affair etc., India had taken a leading part. The results are well known. Subsequent events, particularly to policies of the United States, Britain and China, have marred some of these results.

In regard to Colonialism and Racialism, India as one of the earliest liberated countries pioneered these moves. Today, thanks to the accession of strength to this cause by the joining up of each successive liberated country, the virility of the new African States, the consistent support of the U.S.S.R. and the Eastern European countries and the disintegration of the former empires of France and Britain, the ending of Colonialism is accepted as a principal objective of the United Nations. In regard to Racialism, India was the pioneer at the United Nations against the Racist policies of the Union of South Africa. Today all nations, bar two or three, do not vote against the Afro-Asian countries on Racist issues: only a small few abstain. Portugal and South Africa alone vote against. This is a different story from 1946 when, in the discussions on people of Indian origin in South Africa and in 1955, when the *apartheid* issue was hotly contested by the Western countries, these issues were "saved" for further consideration only by a dexterous procedural handling at the United Nations!

On world issues, mainly disarmament and the prohibition of nuclear arms, India has been in the forefront and been more than once responsible for resolving deadlocks as between the blocs. Indian initiative played a considerable part in bringing about the Eighteen Nation Conference on Disarmament at Geneva when the Disarmament Commission had been stultified.

It comes as ridicule in certain quarters that India has no friends in the world on account of non-alignment and the conduct of her foreign affairs. This arises from a misconception both of non-alignment and friendship. Non-alignment is essentially based upon national independence. A non-aligned country is not part of a bloc and should be expected to take an independent though not necessarily hostile attitude.

It is surprising if not amusing, that this particular criticism, more often than otherwise, comes from persons and quarters who over the years have argued that India should become aligned to the West! With West-made arms and Western diplomacy so increasingly and massively ranged against India and now in action on our frontiers, this plaintiveness is, to say the least, misconceived. . . .

What sticks out a mile is that the allies of our foes are not militarily allied against us. The Western countries are diplomatically ranged against us on Kashmir — Britain from the beginning and the rest from 1949. The allies of China, the U.S.S.R. and the Eastern European allies, have not lifted a finger to help China. They have been on our side in respect of Pakistan despite our less close relations with them than with the West. They have not yet placed embargoes on arms against us. The Soviet Union has consistently sought to understand and assist India.

Large numbers of countries have adopted non-alignment as their policy since 1952. Then India and U Nu's Burma were the only non-aligned countries. Today all the former colonial countries except Pakistan are non-aligned. They do not support our foes.

It is one of the recognised elements of a successful foreign policy that a country obtains the neutrality of others, isolates foes, and prevents combinations against her. This has happened in respect of us. . . .

Furthermore, our non-alignment is understood and welcomed by members of one of the power blocs. The countries of the West have begun to understand it, shifted from their earlier attitudes of ridicule and hostility. They have utilised our non-aligned position in the steps to resolve world problems as in Korea or Indo-China. They have also found it of value in problems where co-operation between the two bloc countries has been essential and in the lowering of world tensions. The United States is not today pronounced in its hostility to non-alignment. Non-alignment has thus provided an "area" (not geographical) of peace in a world where the two blocs are poised against each other.

The second criticism, ill-informed, is that not only are we without [friends], but we have on account of our foreign policy denied ourselves, resources, economic and military, which should be otherwise available to us. This is totally untrue. We have ever since Independence procured military equipment from the countries of the Western bloc and later from those of the East as well. At no time have we taken the position that non-alignment is a self-denying ordinance in this respect. In fact, it is the leaders of the Western bloc who have now succeeded somewhat in imposing this on us: in the past, by being unwilling or unable to release goods to us for so-called security reasons which we have manufactured ourselves in many cases. So far as economic aid is concerned, India has received from both the blocs substantial aid. At the height of the non-alignment controversy, all aid from the West to India was totally devoid of conditions — no strings.

On the contrary, we had ever regarded even the talk of military aid as inconsistent with our policy and contrary to our interests. India abandoned this inhibition under the impact of the betrayal of her by China. The aid which has come to India since then [1962] has been limited in quantum and severely conditioned by the military alliance of the donor countries with Pakistan. Furthermore, the goods of these donors have been available to Pakistan in sizable quantities as against the small dose we received and even after the latter had joined up with China against India. We even permitted our independence and dignity to be denigrated by accepting conditions which have not been imposed by the West on their SEATO ally.

The other instance of our departure from our basic policy has been in regard to PL-480 grain. This is a case by itself. It is an error to call it aid, inasmuch as we pay for the grain, which is surplus in the supplying country.[1] The PL-480 agreement has been proved to be a political weapon. The Prime Minister [Shastri] announced this week (October 16, 1965) in Bombay that we shall not avail ourselves of PL-480 supplies. The recent developments in this matter have demonstrated to our people and government that the critics of PL-480 have been right all along. The consignment has humiliated us, made grave inroads into our fiscal and economic structure, and enabled ominous economic penetration. Furthermore, it will be found and seen enough, that it has affected our agriculture adversely. . . .

But along with PL-480 and the post-

[1] Enacted in 1954, United States Public Law 480 (Food for Peace) authorizes sales at competitive world prices of surplus agricultural products for local currency, saving the purchaser's hard currency. Seventy to eighty percent of the proceeds may be loaned or granted to the recipient for economic development projects; limited amounts are used for United States diplomatic and other expenses in the recipient country and for loans to American firms doing business in the country. The proceeds may not be used to buy the products of the recipient. In India, sizable "blocked" funds have been accumulated under PL-480 transactions and other repayments, chiefly because mutually agreed upon ways have not been found to utilize them internally through "feed back" development loans. During her American visit in 1966, Prime Minister Gandhi and President Johnson announced an agreement to establish an Indo-American educational foundation to aid Indian science and research, financed by blocked funds. Krishna Menon and other Indians objected to the proposal as interventionist, leading to its shelving. Menon told the editor in October 1966 that the blocked funds should be cancelled. [Editor's note.]

China oppression of 1962, military aid and as a consequence of it our economy and economic policies, have suffered denigration. Economic imperialism threatens us and will engulf us unless we extricate ourselves soon enough. Recent policies in the economic and financial spheres and in respect of our industrial and technical development projects have been large-scale surrenders to foreign economic power and to its domination. . . . Our talk of "self-reliance" will be a mockery and further subject us to the scepticism about our integrity if we do not turn sharply away from this reversal of our policy of independence and non-alignment in relation to economic aid and collaboration.[2]

It will thus be seen that it is not non-alignment, but the departure from it that has been prejudicial to our interests. We first gradually and later steeply, succumbed to the pitfall of conditioned aid. Our finance administration in recent times has gone headlong into industrial and economic collaboration terms which are onerous economically, prejudicial in respect of self-reliance and politically inimical to our interests and national independence. Politically the effect of the considerable shift in our economic and developmental alignment, has been to cast long shadows on the image of our independence. Our foes like China have exploited it. Internally, it has aided the forces of monopoly, large profits, foreign control and the denigration of our confidence and personality. . . .

We now turn to the crisis revolutionaries, reformers and sloganists. The cases they advance call for examination if only to clear our own minds. There are those who want a "new policy." This is in reference to foreign policy. If by a "new policy" is meant shifts in tempo, the taking into account of newly emerging factors, or profitting by errors, their own or that of others, it is a welcome outlook. But, quite obviously, what the "prochangers" want is the abandonment of non-alignment. Some of them go to the extent of talking about living down the past, of rescuing the country from the errors of the Nehru era, etc. "New policy"! This is another name for "alignment," dependence and seeking and hoping for strength from others. Alignment in the present context means joining the West, curtailing relations with the Afro-Asian world, turning our back on Indo-Arab friendship. They would like to call it to "negotiate" from strength. Whose strength? Negotiate with whom?

They expect the people to forget that Western arms are pointing at our chest, the policy of the Western alliance is basically unchanged and furthermore that the price of even a modicum of Western co-operation is the surrender of Kashmir and the professed goals of our internal economic policy.

Where has even the limited degree of shift in this direction taken us? They must face the answer provided by recent facts. We face an arms embargo, while Pakistan has arms conduited to it through the CENTO powers. We have the PL-480 weapon pointed at us. We also see that the Sino-Pakistan combination has not brought the Pakistan-West alliances to an end! On

[2] In 1965 when Krishna Menon wrote this article, a severe drought reduced India's food grain production from 88 million tons in the previous crop year to 72 million tons for 1965–66. Led by the United States, a massive international program filled most of the gap. A 1966 drought brought another emergency, causing a search for about 11 million tons for 1967 when domestic production may reach 79 million tons and the United States may place a ceiling on its help. In a special message to Congress in February 1967, President Johnson asked permission to sell 3 million tons of surplus grain to India, with other countries matching the effort. He indicated that the United States would provide food by new sales and emergency measures at least one half of India's likely shortage for 1967. The President stressed the self-help aspect of India's food problem, recounting the Indian government's increased effort to provide incentives for farmers, stimulate fertilizer production with the help of foreign capital, improve transportation and distribution systems and step up family planning. Announcing a new policy based on cost and supply factors and the political drawbacks of bilateralism which Krishna Menon's criticisms illustrate, President Johnson said that henceforth the aid-to-India consortium under the World Bank should have food as well as financial responsibilities. In April 1967 the consortium began to seek a multilateral way to decrease India's food problem. [Editor's note.]

the contrary, Pakistan used CENTO, SEATO and NATO and Chinese resources against us and for all we know continues to do so.

Here is something for the prochangers to think about. To be aligned, even if the United States were prepared to buy our submission, it can only be at the price of (a) isolation from Afro-Asia; (b) total dependence on the West, in effect the United States; (c) abandonment of our social goals; (d) abandonment of the reality of self-reliance; (e) strengthening of the Sino-Pakistan axis. They cannot fail to note that the military ally of the West, whom they seek to join, Pakistan, while still condoned and cajoled, had to face the fact that the Western alliances and weapons have not taken her to her goal of conclusive military value!

Next come those who in a more moderate vein ask for "flexibility." What is non-alignment if it is not flexible? It is flexible because it is a policy of independence and, therefore, nationally determinable. It is flexible because it is based on mutuality of interest. It is flexible because it does not involve ideological commitments to capitalism or communism. It is flexible because it is pragmatic and takes into account the dynamism of change. . . .

Then there are the advocates of dual or plural alignments. But the latter is what non-alignment is! Peaceful co-existence, mutual interest, reciprocity, all these are elements of what the group of reformers or revolutionaries choose to regard as dual or plural alignment.

It does not do, either to rest on one's oars, to chant "non-alignment" or even merely to answer critics. All these have a somewhat defensive, complacent and "stand as you were" tone. This is not the tone we need. Our interests do not lie that way. Furthermore, events pass us by if we disregard them or are blissfully ignorant of them. Ours is a changing world. Our policies have to be dynamic. We are engaged by forces of reaction as well as of progress. Foes threaten our sovereignty. To many a

question posed by the dynamism of change, there may be no simple or straight answer. Yet our postures, our dynamism, must provide answers. They are not eternal in validity. Our interests are. Our duty to them is also eternal. Assessments must take place continuously. . . .

First of all, we should shed fear. We must not leave to Pakistan or China the determining of our policies. This is what would happen if we do not pursue policies which are moved by our interest, conditioned by our history and uninhibited by prejudices. We have to recognize that our defence against Pakistan is not only against her armies, but against pressures from her allies. We should have no delusions that Pakistan will not continue at least for a measurable time as a Western client, despite her courtship with China. Britain, the United States, West Germany, the CENTO should be left in no doubt that our policies cannot be determined by their pressures. We should tell them frankly that Pakistan's military supporters are pointing their guns at us.

But more, the dependence on P.L. 480 was a blunder of the first magnitude. We should undo it. . . . We should put an end to all collaboration agreements that are not primarily and in the long run in India's interests. We need to reassess this doctrine of "attracting foreign capital." We need to banish the superstition that we gain strength by denying its acquisition for ourselves. . . .

The time has come for us to tell all prospective vendors that we [will] pay for goods in rupees; it may sound fantastic to some when so stated. Strange as it may seem, even the United States will understand it after the first shock and come to accept it.[3] She acclimatised herself to non-alignment over a few years even though

[3] Krishna Menon refers to United States willingness to accept Indian currency instead of dollars for American goods. Food sales to India have usually been for rupees, although, in 1966, the prospect of an American insistence on the dollar payment for food sales to all nations began to emerge for the years ahead. [Editor's note.]

she ridiculed and rebuked. The vendor country must buy our goods. Of all the vendor countries, the United States is more likely to do it after the first burst of anger, ridicule and threat. This may sound a drastic change in policy. It may shock the pundits of the [Indian] Reserve Bank and the Finance Ministry. The idea of the indigenous manufacture of arms did the same. They thwarted it. But necessity has now educated them. . . .

In the field of foreign policy, India should not remain inhibited by the shock of Chinese invasion. Her concern about nuclear peril, about disarmament and co-existence must be reactivated. It is not in our interest to permit doubts to be engendered in regard to our declared policy [of opposition to atomic arms] and integrity in respect of the nuclear weapon. . . .

Indo-Arab relations are pivotal to India's foreign policy. Arab-Indian solidarity is a necessary constituent in the stability of both our continents. The West should be inhibited from playing at power politics in our areas. In Africa, our earlier relationships arising from our identification with their fight for liberation must now be replaced by our sharing with them the struggle for the liberation of the rest of the colonial world. The erasing of racial inequality must be felt by Africa and by us with equal concern. The Organisation of African Unity has surprised all the world by its emergence as also by its cohesion.

The role of the Soviet Union as a great Asian and world power is of primary and overwhelming significance to us. She does not seek to make us aligned, and has never done so. The U.A.R. has drawn closer to the U.S.S.R. This should be a lesson. There is no attempt at domination of us by the U.S.S.R. We should have no fear of it. Our relations with the U.S.S.R. have to assume a more normal and different pattern, and be of richer content. In any large scale industrial advance of India, the Soviet Union has to play a conclusive role many times larger and more diverse than at present. Indo-Soviet relations must reflect dynamism on both sides. This should be on a more permanent basis. This will help the West to understand us better and help towards a world of greater equality.

China's relations with us will undergo change with greater Indo-Soviet solidarity. The U.S.S.R. must feel that we are common Asian nations and that our attraction to her is not only because she is a rupee area. China's willingness to be a good neighbour to India is to a certain extent dependent upon her learning this, if need be, the hard way. If the U.S.S.R. and India adopt the outlook of world States devoid of the desire to dominate, bound by ties of mutual respect and interest, the forces of world co-operation will be on the way to winning.

The idea that the United States and the U.S.S.R. have come closer together and that the relation of the latter with India will be shared by her with the United States in a two party arrangement is an error. The Soviet Union's interest in India and her relations with India will not be channelled through the United States or conditioned by her. Our friendship with the Soviet Union need not detract from our developing and maintaining good relations with the United States. Indeed, this will become more possible with greater normality in Indo-Soviet relations. The United States will then take her place in the world as one of the great powers whose function is dependent on the trust and goodwill of the developing countries. It is in her long term interest to let Soviet relations with the Asian and African countries grow so that they become active partners in the endeavour for world peace.

Today, China and Pakistan quite naturally condition a disproportionate share of our thinking. Greater strength, arising from self-reliance, a higher standard of life, and growth of technology to which the U.S.S.R. can contribute more than any other State will help towards a Sino-Indian equilibrium. The normalisation of relations with China, which must come, can only happen when Indo-Soviet relations disable

China from holding up India as an imperial puppet or a field for expansionism.

In these and other ways rethinking is required. We need courage not only to defend our territorial frontier, but to dare to think in new dimensions. We need to be potent to help in building the bridges that will lead to a greater unity in the world. Our internal strength and our external relations have to develop further. Our nationalism must venture on its next long leap. It shall not be in the dark but illumined by our experience of the recent past, the wisdom that was Nehru's and the imaginativeness and the courage that must be ours alone.

Nonalignment Without Myth

M. S. RAJAN

An authority on Commonwealth affairs, M. S. Rajan is Director of the Indian School of International Studies in New Delhi. In this selection, he offers a major restatement of nonalignment. Conceding that nonalignment can no longer be a moral imperative, he criticizes Nehru's thought and practice. Affirming that the country's national interest requires a continuation of nonalignment, he argues that it must persist as a strategy. Power realities concern him as they do Michael Edwardes, although Rajan does not believe that India will be unable to refashion its foreign policy because of Nehru's tradition. He endorses a strong military position to replace the policy of deterrence through friendship found in Nehru's China policy. Calling for self-assurance, he reformulates nonalignment as a peacemaking force which is traditional in purpose but revised in rationale and means.

UNTIL very recently all the parties of the Left, Right and Centre supported the policy of non-alignment. The criticism of the Government related only to concrete cases of implementation. The one major theme of criticism of all the Opposition parties, with the exception of the Communist Party, was that, in operation, the policy was partial to the Communist bloc and unduly critical of the Western bloc.

The question naturally arises whether any or all of the . . . reasons for India following the policy of non-alignment still hold good after Chinese aggression, and whether any change in this respect is called for. It seems to the present writer that none of the basic and standing reasons for adopting non-alignment, and practising it so far, is irrelevant or inapplicable to India after Chinese aggression. On the other hand, the situation both within India, and the world in which she finds herself after Chinese aggression, emphatically calls for no other policy. Indeed, one could even go so far as to argue that, in the present situation, it is all the more necessary to hold on to the same anchor of non-alignment to preserve as well as promote our vital national interests. Those who have been

From M. S. Rajan, "Chinese Aggression and the Future of India's Non-Alignment Policy," *International Studies*, 5 (July–October 1963), 118–132, selections. Reprinted by permission.

demanding in recent weeks a change in policy are basing their demands either on unproved hypotheses or on an erroneous understanding of non-alignment as a policy.

Thus, some critics have suggested that China dared to commit aggression on India precisely because she was non-aligned, and in order to destroy the success of non-alignment as a valid and practical policy in international affairs. They cite in support of their view Mao Tse-tung's repeated statements that a country could belong *either* to the "socialist camp" *or* to the "imperialist camp" and that there was no third choice. It is said that the Chinese were jealous of the success of our non-alignment, that they felt especially chagrined that we were benefiting from economic assistance from both Communist and non-Communist camps, that they believed that we were not genuinely non-aligned and wanted therefore to expose our alleged *de facto* alignment with the Western bloc, and that, in fact, their object in attacking us was to push us into the Western camp so as to deny us the benefits of economic assistance from the Communist camp.

But, surely, nobody knows why the Chinese sought to commit aggression on India; there must have been a variety of reasons, and perhaps the desire to destroy our non-alignment was not the most crucial of them. The claim that our following the policy of non-alignment is the reason which encouraged the Chinese to commit aggression, can only be one of the many hypotheses. It also seems difficult to believe that the Chinese would have chosen such a costly instrument as a major invasion of India merely to expose our alleged alignment with the West. They must have anticipated that driving us into the Western camp would lead to the very opposite and most unwelcome result of militarily strengthening us against China with Western assistance.

Acharya [J. B.] Kripalani has advanced the view that, since India is the victim of aggression by a member of the Communist bloc, we can no longer claim to be non-aligned. This is over-simplifying the issue. It is now too well known that China is not a member of the Communist bloc in the same sense as, say, Czechoslovakia — in spite of the Sino-Soviet Treaty of Friendship, Alliance and Mutual Assistance of 1950. Secondly, we know now that all members of the Communist bloc (including China, ostensibly though) continue to recognize and respect non-alignment as a valid policy for India as well as other Asian-African countries. Thirdly, excepting possibly North Korea, North Vietnam and Albania, all the rest of the Communist countries (including Yugoslavia) have criticized (though not quite explicitly or sharply as most of the Western countries) the Chinese action against India. Furthermore, the Communist parties of most non-Communist countries of the world (including the Communist Party of India) have done likewise. Hence, Prime Minister Nehru is quite right in pointing out that what we are up against is *Chinese* expansionism — not *Communist* expansionism.

It is, therefore, hardly correct to say that we are no longer non-aligned in "cold war" politics after the Chinese aggression. And it may be added, that those Western nations who are now giving us military assistance to repel Chinese aggression, have not only *not* asked us to join the Western camp in view of the aid, but have, on the contrary, also public expressed their support to our non-alignment. Also, it is known that after the recent Chinese aggression, India appealed for military assistance to the Soviet Union at the same time as she did for Western help. If the Soviet Union has not responded to our appeal by any significant supply of military equipment (apart from supplying some helicopters on deferred payment), it is not our fault. It must be assumed that if the Soviet Government was afraid that our getting substantial military assistance from the Western camp was likely to compromise our non-alignment, they themselves would have offered similarly substantial aid. . . .

A like criticism has been that since the

Soviet Union has, so far as we know, done nothing to discourage, and much less to prevent, Chinese aggression on us, or since the Soviet Government has not publicly supported our stand on the border dispute, or categorically and fully sympathized with our military reverses (while the Western Governments had done so), there is no point in our continuing the policy of non-alignment. It is said that in order to get the full benefit of the Western support against a possible renewal of war with China, we should give up non-alignment and join the Western camp.

It is true that millions of Indians were deeply disappointed that the Soviet Union did not either come out openly on our side after the October-November 1962 Chinese aggression, or openly and categorically condemn China for her attack on India. However, this view ignores the patent fact that China continues to be a military ally of the Soviet Union and that the Soviet Union cannot (in order to oblige us) treat China as Stalinist Russia did Yugoslavia, or as another Albania today. It is possible that the Soviet Union is marking steps in the ideological dispute with Peking in the hope that the final break could be postponed for as long as possible. Presumably, it is thought that a final break with China is too grave a matter for the other Communist countries to take any precipitate action. It is too much for Indians to expect that Soviet sympathies and support to India in our conflict with China should go so far as to denounce publicly a fellow Communist country. Until the Sino-Soviet ideological rift leads to a break between the two Communist giants, we should be content with Soviet neutrality in the Sino-Indian border conflict and accept at their face value Soviet assurances of respect for our non-alignment. Since Soviet assurances are accompanied by continuing Soviet economic (and even military, like the supply of some MIG aircraft and commitment to build in India a MIG aircraft factory) assistance to India (as well as that of other Central European Communist states), it

would be imprudent on our part to give up non-alignment out of mere peevishness against the Soviet Union.

It is not only unwise, but positively dangerous to give up our non-alignment in the context of our relations with the Soviet Union. By doing so, we would undoubtedly incur the full force of displeasure of the Soviet Union and other East and Central European states — and it may be noted that the Soviet Union is our northern neighbour. Even beyond this; we would also thereby cease to enjoy the goodwill and friendship of other non-aligned countries of the world. Even though not all non-aligned countries have supported us in the conflict with China, it would surely be unwise to incur the displeasure of *all* of them, which we would, if we gave up non-alignment. And this would not only confirm persistent Chinese propaganda that we have not been genuinely non-aligned all these years, but also give them an additional and dangerous handle against India in the rest of the world.

If we ever have to give up non-alignment, it would only be in favour of aligning with the Western bloc; in the present context at least, it is impossible to conceive otherwise. If this is so, what is the attitude of the Western bloc to the possibility of our aligning with it? If the Soviet Union has not, ever since it officially recognized our non-alignment in 1955, wanted us to give up our non-alignment and to align with the Communist bloc, today the Western bloc (which was once so critical of our non-alignment) is quite understanding and appreciative of it. More: the United States authorities in particular are not at all eager (as they once were) to annex any more allies in the "cold war" and would probably be unwilling to ask for, or accept, any further military alliances, because they no longer need them for their security against the presumed threat of the Communist bloc. Because of the revolution in weapon technology and the means of their delivery, the Western countries, more especially the United States, no longer need military allies or land bases around the periphery of the Communist bloc. The United States authorities now seem to consider even their present allies quite dispensable and burdensome financially, some of whom could be easily dropped off without in the least adversely affecting American and Western security. Therefore, those like Mr. Rajagopalachari[1] who argue in favour of our seeking a firm military alliance with the West in the context of the "permanent menace" from China are doing so in vain. The West is not waiting with open arms to receive India into its bosom. If we seek such an alliance in panic, the likelihood is that we would be rebuffed.

Some critics . . . have been asserting that we have already compromised our non-alignment in favour of the West (because of the acceptance of Western arms aid). . . . Mr. Jayaprakash Narayan[2] has expressed satisfaction that we are now no longer non-aligned in favour of the Communist bloc mentally and emotionally, as he says we were before the Chinese aggression, and that, therefore, there need be no further controversy as to the validity of non-alignment as a policy for India. Mr. Rajagopalachari has been further arguing that since our present policy is oriented to the West, we might as well formally ally ourselves with the West. If we do not, says he, while, on the one hand, we would not get the full benefit of alignment with the West; on the other hand, we would be incurring the suspicions of the Communist bloc as to the genuineness of our non-alignment; he also suggests that, between the two blocs, by aligning with the West we will be more honest in our relations.

1 Chakravarti Rajagopalachari was a close associate of Gandhi and after freedom served as India's terminal Governor-General. In 1959 he helped to establish the anti-collectivist Swatantra party and became a critic of the Nehru government's foreign and domestic policies. [Editor's note.]
2 An independent critic and theorist who is difficult to classify, Jayaprakash Narayan is an advocate of "partyless politics" and a decentralized society. A former Marxist, he was influenced by Gandhi and his teachings and in the mid-1950s was considered a possible successor to Nehru. [Editor's note.]

All this criticism is unconvincing. Two things are quite clear. We have not compromised (as Yugoslavia has not) non-alignment by the acceptance of Western aid. . . . Equally, both the blocs continue to recognize our non-alignment. Whether we were non-aligned in favour of the Communist bloc before, and are aligned in favour of the Western bloc now, is a matter of opinion, depending upon the ideological disposition of the critics, not on any objective facts. . . .

It is said by some critics that the avowed respect for our non-alignment, presently being shown by the leaders of both the blocs, is insincere and opportunistic, meant to lull us into deception — and that either of them would at some appropriate time in the future go back on their present stand and try to annex India as an ally. Therefore, it is suggested by these critics, we now make up our minds as to which bloc is sincerely friendly — and, according to these critics, it is the Western bloc, as demonstrated by the readiness with which it responded to our appeal for military assistance against Chinese aggression — and align with it in order to ensure our future security.

A student of diplomatic history could, however, point out that, in international relations, the only permanent factor is the interests of a nation, and not friendships and enmities which are of a transient character, and any nation which relies wholly on its friendships (or, for that matter, enmities) to promote its national interests is bound to be surprised and disillusioned sooner or later (as India has been vis-a-vis China). Secondly, there is no way of proving or disproving whether either of the blocs today is sincere or not in its professions of respect for non-alignment, and the past does not give us any guide to the future. Until about 1955, the Communist bloc did not accept our non-alignment as genuine — it considered it a mere facade for our de facto alignment with the West. Indeed, it went further in not categorically acknowledging our independence. Likewise, until very recently, the Western bloc did not acknowledge the integrity of our non-alignment policy; it thought that our policy was inclined in favour of the Communist bloc and was even "immoral." Both the blocs are now pretty vociferous about their respect for our non-alignment policy, but nobody can say with any certainty that either of them is sincere in its stand. All that one can say with certainty is that their present attitude to non-alignment is simply in furtherance of their permanent national interests as *now* conceived.

It is clear that in the existing nuclear stalemate, when both the blocs have ceased to be monolithic as they once were (with deep divisions within both the camps), with the tempo of "cold war" lessened and the two groups moving into a *detente* with no more need for military allies to ensure their security, the non-aligned countries have ceased to be important (and indeed become largely irrelevant) to their competitive needs of security against the other bloc. This is a welcome development, in so far as the non-aligned countries have now practically ceased to be pawns in the "cold war" political chess. Therefore, *a fortiori*, it seems that India could continue to be non-aligned without the erstwhile threat to her policy from either of the blocs, and irrespective of the sincerity or otherwise of their attitudes to non-alignment. To abandon the policy just when, at last, both the blocs respect it, seems a little absurd on the face of it.

One other reason being given by critics of non-alignment in urging its abandonment is that it holds no guarantee against aggression. It is pointed out that no Communist state has so far dared to commit aggression against a country aligned with the Western bloc. And, perhaps, pro-Communists could equally argue that the West has not dared to commit aggression on a nation aligned with the Communist bloc. The British Prime Minister, Harold Macmillan, and the Japanese Prime Minister, Ikeda, reinforced this view by stating recently that Chinese aggression on India demonstrated that "neutrality" was no guarantee against aggression and that

"neutralism" was unrealistic as a policy in international affairs.

This is one more instance of over-simplifying the nature and working of international politics and of taking a mechanistic view of international affairs, apart from showing ignorance of diplomatic history. Nothing is a guarantee against anything in the world as it is today. Belgian neutrality did not prevent German aggression against it during the first World War. On the other hand, was not Swiss neutrality respected by all the belligerents during both the World Wars?

Furthermore, non-alignment or international guarantees of neutrality *as such* are no guarantee, always and for ever, against aggression, and it is clearly wrong for anybody to claim, as our foreign-policy makers did sometimes, that it is so. On the contrary, alignment is not also, always and necessarily, a guarantee against aggression; for anybody to think so, is as illusory as in believing that non-alignment would give a similar guarantee. Those who think that alignment secures firm friends for any state should ponder over the pithy remark of the present Pakistani Minister for External Affairs, Z. A. Bhutto, made some weeks ago (when he was still the Minister of Industries): "India finds herself friendless because of non-alignment, and Pakistan finds herself friendless because of membership of military pacts.". . .

It is clear, therefore, that it is quite prudent, profitable and even necessary that we stick to the moorings of non-alignment as closely as before. We have everything to gain by doing so. We would gain nothing more by aligning with the Western bloc. On the contrary, it might be positively dangerous to give it up.

All this is not to say that in previous years the Indian Government has not committed any mistakes in formulating or implementing foreign policy which (among other things) might have encouraged the Chinese to mount an attack against India. The present writer maintains, however, that these mistaken policies and actions have no inevitable and necessary connexion with the policy of non-alignment as such. Thus, for instance, until now the Government seemed to base its policies and actions in world affairs, and in particular in relation to China, on the unwarranted assumption that non-alignment as such was a safeguard against any threat to our security — that merely because we were non-aligned with either of the blocs of the "cold war," China would not, or dare not, threaten our security and territorial integrity. On this erroneous assumption, among others, the Government seems to have neglected our defence *vis-a-vis* China.

It is hardly necessary to point out that non-alignment has nothing to do with the nature of defence preparedness of a country, and that it does not mean that a country can afford to neglect its defences; vice versa, the building of defensive strength does not violate non-alignment. The conclusive examples of this are those of Yugoslavia and Egypt (also Indonesia in recent years) which have built up strong defensive strength with the help of American and Soviet Governments, respectively, without at the same time giving up their non-alignment with the two blocs of the "cold war," headed by their military donors. They have also demonstrated effectively that the receipts of foreign military aid, even from the leaders of the two blocs of the "cold war," does not necessarily and inevitably compromise their countries' non-alignment in the bloc politics, as the Indian Government has been erroneously asserting for many years. If such comparatively small countries as Yugoslavia and Egypt could retain their non-alignment in spite of receiving military aid from the leaders of the two blocs, there was no reason at all why India should have feared any adverse impact on our non-alignment of military assistance from either of the blocs.

Even if we were opposed to receiving foreign military aid for sentimental and psychological reasons, we could surely have built up our defensive strength by allocating far more of our internal resources to defence than we have been doing until the

Chinese aggression.[3] This would have, of course, impeded our socio-economic development — though at the same time it would have strengthened the industrial base of our economy in support of defence industries. But that is the price all nations have to pay in this world of sovereign nations (in the absence of adequate collective security arrangements) for safeguarding their independence and territorial integrity. The single most important lesson of our recent military reverses against China is, that because we tried to economize on defence expenditure and concentrated on building up a welfare society, we could not adequately safeguard our territorial integrity. . . . While there could be no objection to foreign military aid as such, we should try to avoid depending too much on it by increasing our internal sources which we have so far not done adequately. The Chinese have now left us no alternative but to augment our military strength to match theirs up to a degree. But since too much dependence on the West is likely to compromise our non-alignment, we should do so largely from internal sources. Logically, this would call for our giving up the present self-denying ordinance in respect of manufacturing nuclear weapons (which Mr. Nehru continues to reaffirm even after Chinese aggression) since (according to press reports) China is likely to make its first atomic bombs during the next two-three years. Obviously, we cannot, and should not, rely permanently on the protection of either the West or the Soviet Union against the Chinese threat of "atomic blackmail" (as the Chinese now call the Western military posture), for that

3 According to the comparative statistical study of defence expenditure made by a UN Expert group on economic and social consequences of disarmament for the years 1957–59, India's expenditure was only 2.4 per cent of the gross domestic product. The comparative figures for some other non-aligned countries are as follows: Burma, 7.3; Cambodia, 4.0; Ceylon, 1.0; Indonesia, 4.6; Lebanon, 3.0; Syria, 5.6; Yugoslavia, 9.0; Sweden, 4.7; Switzerland, 3.0. (Source: UN Doc. E/3593/Rev. I, Table 2-1.) In the 1963–64 budget, our defence expenditure has gone up to a little less than 6 per cent. [Author's note.]

would eventually compromise our non-alignment.

Unfortunately, our policy-makers seemed to have believed until now that a strong military establishment was incompatible with non-alignment; or, to put it the other way, that non-alignment necessarily meant keeping a relatively weak military establishment, presumably (and among other reasons) under the mistaken belief that augmenting our peace-time military establishment might provoke our aligned and un-aligned neighbours and tarnish our world image as a peace-loving nation. That this need not be so, has been amply demonstrated by non-aligned, but militarily strong, Switzerland, Yugoslavia and Egypt.

In the minds of some of our Congress leaders, non-alignment seems to have been confused with non-violence with which weapon we fought our struggle for freedom. Of course, the Government of India has never been a devotee of non-violence, but the minds of many of the Congress leaders seem to have been clouded by their memory of the effectiveness of non-violence against British rule, resulting in a conscious as well as unconscious resistance to large-scale defence expenditure. There is, however, absolutely no correlation between non-alignment and non-violence. The two ideas belong to two altogether different categories of thought — the former is a political policy, the latter a moral principle.

Another mistake our foreign-policy makers seem to have committed is to confuse non-alignment, which is merely an instrument of our policy, for the very goals of our foreign policy, or to treat it as a moral imperative from which no deviation is permissible except under moral obloquy. The ultimate goal of our foreign policy, like that of any other country, is to promote our enlightened national interests, and we sought to achieve it by following the policy of non-alignment, among others. This meant that if and when non-alignment ceased to promote our national interests (that situation has not yet arisen), we ought to switch on to any of the other alternative courses of policy available to us at any time, without being charged with political expediency. But the Government has treated the policy all along as not just a means to promote our national interests, but as the end itself. . . .

They also treated the policy of non-alignment as a fetish to worship and as a saviour of the country. It was treated as a sacred cow which ought not to be touched by anybody else, even by a friendly critic of the Government. It is completely misleading to say, as Prime Minister Nehru said recently, that if we abandon non-alignment it would mean a "terrible moral failure." To treat it as a moral principle is wholly an error; it is simply a political policy which happens to have paid ample dividends to us as well as to many Asian-African countries. To consider it as a moral precept is to commit the same mistake as John Foster Dulles once did when he called "neutralism" immoral. Furthermore, as Acharya Kripalani wrote recently, if non-alignment is sought to be treated by the Government as a moral imperative, then it, as well as the nation, must be ready to suffer martyrdom in its cause (as Gandhiji was willing to do for the sake of non-violence). To point to this logical consequence of treating it as a moral imperative is to underline its absurdity.

This attitude towards non-alignment is in turn due to another, and a related, weakness of our foreign policy. Due partly to this unbounded faith in non-alignment, and partly to the exaggerated emphasis on idealism and ethical principles in the conduct of international relations, we seem to have become often slaves to a doctrinal, crusading approach to international problems. In an imperfect world, in a world which is not wholly governed even by the principles of international law, let alone ethical principles, it is sheer fool-hardiness on our part to rely entirely on the self-executing goodness of idealistic principles, not backed by military strength. To have faith in *panchsheel* is all to the good, but to rely wholly on its efficacy is dangerous in an imperfect community of nations. We should have at the same time built up sufficient military strength which would have proved a bulwark in case of violation of the *panchsheel* — and the two concurrent approaches would not have been inconsistent, as noted earlier. Even Hitler respected Swiss neutrality, but not wholly because of any respect for it as such, but also (and *inter alia*) because that brave little country backed it up with substantial military strength. . . .

It seems to me, therefore, that no "agonizing reappraisal" of our policy of non-alignment is called for in view of the Chinese aggression. What is most certainly called for is a reappraisal of our attitude to, and relations with, certain countries of both the blocs of the "cold war" and even some non-aligned countries. This reappraisal we can easily make without altering the basic principles of our foreign policy, and without incurring any moral obloquy. At least, in the present context, we would gain nothing by aligning ourselves with any bloc, not even with the Western bloc. And the West does not want us to do so. And the Soviet Union is also respecting our non-alignment, and certainly does not expect us to align ourselves with the Communist bloc. Should, however, the Soviet Union openly back Chinese aggression and the Sino-Soviet military alliance come into operation, then, of course, we may be left with no choice but an outright alignment with the Western bloc; and the Soviet Union cannot then blame us for doing so. Until then, it would not only be not desirable and necessary to give up our non-alignment, but it may be dangerous to do so, since, thereby, we would be incurring instantaneously the hostility of the entire Communist bloc, including the Soviet Union. As for the future, let us leave it to international developments to guide our course. Prime Minister Nehru rightly said in a B.B.C. television interview some weeks ago that India would continue non-alignment "subject to one fact — that war conditions create their own momentum." That is the only right posture for the future.

Let us not give up too easily and in panic (and unless and until our national survival is the compelling alternative) the non-alignment which is our proud contribution to the theory of international affairs — something which has contributed to the stature and self-respect of many nations, including ourselves; something which has significantly contributed to the maintenance and promotion of international peace and security. Let us not lose faith in ourselves, our basic convictions and policies, because of the shock of Chinese aggression. Loss of faith in oneself is the beginning of the end of disaster. Besides, what is involved here is more than India's own survival as a sovereign, independent and self-respecting nation. If we who originated this policy of non-alignment, and practised it with demonstrative success, abandon the policy, the faith of more than a score of other nations who have emulated our example is likely to be shaken in their own non-alignment policy. And this in turn, and in due course, is likely to draw these nations into the political and military orbits of the Communist and non-Communist blocs of nations and thereby revive the erstwhile race of the two blocs for allies from among the non-aligned countries. And the revival of the trend towards total bipolarization of the community of nations would once again envelop the world with the threat of a Third World War.

IV. TWO SUMMARY STATEMENTS

Indian Nonalignment and the Balance of Power

A. P. RANA

Few theories of foreign policy are more durable than those of the balance of power. Carefully defined as "responsible," a balance of power theory is used in this commentary on Indian nonalignment as the basis to evaluate its objectives and performance. A. P. Rana, who is Reader in Political Science at Baroda University, finds that India has employed a normative balancing policy without acknowledging the fact and in competition with an ideology of nonalignment, which has often denied it. Relating the normative theory to his interpretation of the impact of nuclear weapons on the interstate system, Rana suggests that India's nonalignment should be viewed as a force which serves to protect its independence and contributes to the preservation of the international community on ethical grounds. In his analysis, he offers ideas employed by both critics and defenders of nonalignment. His presentation also blends "idealistic" and "realistic" viewpoints, a division that crosses the line between critics and defenders. Valuable as an example of how it is possible to comprehend more than one version of nonalignment in a single interpretation, the selection helps to place the study of Indian nonalignment within a major theoretical school of international politics.

ANYONE who is engaged in the study of International Relations is confronted by a concept which, in many ways, is central to this study — the concept of the balance of power. In India, however, this concept has received scant attention. In fact, after independence, we assumed that by being non-aligned we had rejected balance of power policies; that it was our duty to indicate to the great Powers the dangers and futility of pursuing such policies, and of ourselves scrupulously avoiding any taint of them.

Yet we were critical of a phenomenon we had not conceptually attempted to define or understand. Undoubtedly, men in power do not have much time to make subtle distinctions and arrive at fine definitions. Nehru could not be bothered to clarify in his mind what it was he was denigrating. The curious fact, however, was the extent to which Indian scholars accepted many of Nehru's pronouncements without adequately questioning them. Indian scholarship of those years reads so much like toeing of the official line. Indeed, this trend has continued even in the post-Nehru period. Policies of nonalignment and policies of the balance of power have come to be regarded as antithetical in the run of the literature on India's foreign affairs. The implication often is that the great powers are engaged in pursuing balance of power policies,

From A. P. Rana, "The Nature of India's Foreign Policy," *India Quarterly*, 22 (April–June 1966), 101–102, 104, 110–114, 116–117, 120–123, 125–134, selections. Reprinted by permission.

93

whilst we have steadfastly refused to subscribe to them. It would appear that even as scholars, we have been interested, not in critically appraising the official line on foreign affairs, but in being strenuous apologists in its behalf.

To a remarkable degree, the supposedly antithetical relationship between policies of non-alignment and policies of the balance of power, recalls similar identifications in the American attitude to European affairs before 1914 and after 1919. President Wilson, who wanted his country to participate fully in international affairs, spoke of "the great game, now for ever discredited, of the Balance of Power," in a speech on 11 February 1918. President Wilson had famous European predecessors in Bright, Cobden and Kant. . . .

By "balance of power" I mean a process (which I shall call the "balancing process") for the "division" of power available to sovereign states in their external relations *inter se*, through the mechanism of a particular system (which I shall call the "balance system"); this system-managed process, if objectively perceived, has operated by and large (roughly since the 16th century) to preserve the "notional structure" of international society as it emerged during the Renaissance and the Reformation. After 1946, however, the balancing process has operated to preserve not only the "notional structure" but the "physical roots" of this society as well. . . .

. . . Now *all* states necessarily "practice" or "make use of" a balance policy in an international state-system the operative process of which is the balancing process. But there are some states which not only *practice* balance policies but truly *follow* them; and there are others who practice or make use of balance policies so as to tend to or to ultimately *destroy* the balancing process, as we have defined it, or to supersede it. Those who wish to destroy the balancing process or *tend* in that direction, and those who wish to supersede it, are not, however, truly following balance policies, although for the moment they may be practicing or making use of them

Communist China to-day is a particularly apt example. One reason for its strong opposition to non-alignment (especially as practiced by a relatively large power as India) is due to the fact that her policy is not truly a balance policy, whereas India's is very much so. A state which truly, or let us say, a state which normatively, follows a balance policy is a state which sincerely believes, as far as circumstances allow, in preserving its integrity and independence *within* an international society of independent sovereign states. The policies of most of the states belonging to the Commonwealth of Nations are examples of such policies. They are no doubt policies pursuing the national interest, but a larger view of the national interest is taken, and the ultimate connection between the national interest and the interests of the society of states is, as far as possible, kept in mind. Nehru's speeches bear rich evidence of such an attitude to international affairs:

Therefore, whether a country is imperialist or socialist or communist, its foreign minister thinks primarily of the interests of that country. But there is a difference, of course. Some people may think of the interests of their country, regardless of other consequences. Others may think that in the long-term policy the interests of another country is as important to them as that of their own country. . . . self-interest may itself demand a policy of co-operation with other nations, goodwill for other nations. . . . Again, I hope we have still enough moral fibre and spirit left in us to face any danger, not only on the borders of our country but far away, if we think it is a danger to the world; The Commonwealth represents, I hope, not only these democratic institutions but, in a considerable measure, *the content of democracy*. . . . (Italics added). . . . Democracy, in other words, is peaceful co-existence, not only between those who are like each other, but also between those who are unlike each other.

Often, genuine Asian and African anti-colonialism qualifies as a true or normative balance policy, whereas neo-colonialism or international communism or fascism does not. Once again Mr. Nehru may be quoted

.... the fact of it is that even before our eyes we see certain areas where colonialism continues, and is trying to dig itself in, or sometimes changes its shape, putting on new clothes, or putting on a new look, and yet essentially remaining the same thing.

It would be a difficult matter to prove definitively that Nehru saw the United States system of alliances as a neo-colonialist power drive, though sometimes he appeared to give that impression. It is, however, as likely that he feared that without some opposition to the United States of America, from a fairly important state such as India, a drive which might not have originated as an offensive power-drive might degenerate into one. Nehru indirectly voiced this fear often:

We are convinced that there is a keen desire on the part of Asian countries to work together, to confer together. . . . Possibly this is due to a certain resentment against the behaviour of Europe in the past. It is also due, undoubtedly, to a feeling that the Asian countries might still be exploited or dominated by Europe or the countries elsewhere.

and on another occasion he said much more succinctly:

SEATO and the Baghdad Pact, apart from being basically in the wrong direction, affect us intimately. In a sense, they tend to encircle us.

Yet the historical record points to the United States as a Power which, in two world wars, and in the peace treaties which followed them, pursued truly normative balance of power policies. Non-alignment of a large state like India in the circumstances of the post war, nuclear world, has similar characteristics. However, this should not be taken to mean that conflict between truly normative balance policies can be ruled out. Geographical considerations, if none other, make possible such conflicts, (though undoubtedly these will not be as fundamental as the conflict between them and the policies of a Power like Communist China). This, in fact, is the way in which the balancing process has normally worked in the past, notably in the 18th century,

and is likely to continue to work in the future.

This analysis helps in understanding the rationale of Indian non-alignment. It has two essential purposes to serve. On the one hand it is implicitly, though not explicitly, on the side of those Powers who wish to remain independent and sovereign within a society of sovereign states. At the same time, on another plane, policies of non-alignment seek to protect their states from the adverse consequences of the balancing process, consequences which led, for example, to the Partitions of Poland. To turn to Mr. Nehru again, he said in the Lok Sabha on 25 March 1957:

It seems to me to really lead to the conclusion that where circumstances compel an imperialist power to withdraw, necessarily you must presume that it has left a vacuum. If so, how is that vacuum to be filled? Surely if somebody else comes in, it is a repetition of the old story, perhaps in a different form. It can only be filled by the people of that country growing and developing themselves economically, politically, or otherwise.

As explained earlier, even those states who genuinely follow balance policies will come in conflict with each other because the balancing process works through the balance system of individual self-help and self-defence. One has to be wary not only of a hegemonial power like Communist China but also of a power which is not hegemonial by nature (or in history) but may become so through force of circumstances. "In international affairs," said Nehru, "one can never be dead certain, and the friends of today might be enemies of tomorrow." Thus non-alignment whilst protecting a state from the hegemonial tendencies of a hegemonial power, helps also in putting pressure on that state which in its fight against the hegemonial power, might feel obliged to become hegemonial itself. It opposes both the "natural" hegemonist and the "helpless" one; and this is especially necessary because today the fight between the two is a battle of Titans involving the fate of every part of the world.

Seen in this light, there was hardly any contradiction in this country taking Western help when attacked by a hegemonial power like China, whilst continuing to oppose any marked extension of Western influence in Asia, especially in the immediate vicinity of India, (e.g. our recent protest against Western projects of building military bases in the Indian Ocean).

Indian non-alignment, therefore, is not entirely a shoddy affair, although in international affairs no concept or policy can altogether escape that charge. As a concept it has subtlety and richness; and the policies which derive from it are eminently respectable, not only helping this large country to maintain its independence, but also helping international society to continue as a society of independent, sovereign, co-existing states; and this at a time, when that society has expanded enormously and yet bears more soft spots than during any of its past historical phases. Much of this help is effected without economic power and a military capability absurdly limited for such large objectives. Nehru himself pointed this out:

If we have been successful in some measure, the success has been due not obviously to any kind of military strength or financial power, but because we took a correct view of events. If I may say so in all modesty, we understood them more correctly than others, because we were more in tune with the spirit of the age.

He went on to say:

I can understand, although I would not approve, military alliances between Great Powers. That would have some meaning. But to attach small countries to themselves in alliance means — and I say so with all respect to those countries — that they are becoming very much dependent on those countries. . . .

At some stage in the development of the international state-system, it must have appeared vital to politically-minded men (men interested in ordering mankind in the mass) to adopt, however unconsciously, the notion of the idea of "sovereignty" of a particular portion of the earth's surface in relation to another, just as to our remote ancestors it must have seemed expedient to invent the notion of time. Thus the present international state-system, composed as it is of sovereign states, is essentially a *notional* system. It owes its existence to ideas in the minds of men — the idea of state sovereignty, the notion of law governing the inter-relationship between these sovereignties and so on. When a state defends its territory, it is in essence defending an ordering concept in the minds of its rulers and its people; an ordering concept, because the idea of state sovereignty, through mutual recognition, has brought into existence a certain system with particular rules of its own, and has made relations between populated parts of the world, more predictable, more rational and more orderly. Had the fiction of sovereignty not been adopted, and subsequently defended with zeal and devotion through the centuries, the world would have been infinitely more barbarous than it is today.

Therefore, when we say that the balancing process has worked to preserve the structure of this state-system, what we really mean is that the process has worked to uphold and defend an idea, a notion, a fiction. But before the invention of nuclear weapons, even the most violent wars never posed a threat to the "physical roots" (*i.e.* developed land surfaces and human population) of this notional state-system; it did not pose a threat of the physical extinction of these foundations. During the Napoleonic Wars or during Hitler's war, what was threatened was the extinction of the notion of the state-system, not the extinction of human population and developed land surfaces. Napoleon and Hitler were bent on a hegemonial system, but the instruments with which they tried to achieve their purposes did not pose a threat of annihilating the physical foundations of the notional system. Had this been so, their wars would have appeared, even if prospectively successful, to be self-defeating.

Nuclear weapons, however, have made such annihilation possible. Thus the balancing process has now to perform a dual function, which it did not have to perform before. *Whereas before 1945 it had succeeded in preserving the notion of the state-system, now it is being called upon to preserve the physical foundations of that system as well.* No doubt it is the balancing process itself which makes possible such destruction: and this, in fact, is the most potent criticism against the balance of power in the nuclear age. Before 1945, if the balancing process had failed, the state-system of sovereign states might have suffered eclipse but not land surfaces and the human race: these would have continued to exist even under a hegemonial system. But if the balancing process, which we have identified with the balance of power, were to fail in the nuclear age, the human race itself would perish and together with it all the notions and systems of organising and ordering human society on an international scale.

This makes it all the more imperative that we correctly understand and appreciate the functioning of the balance of power in our times, in order to enable it to work normatively, rather than destructively.[1] . . .

. . . The balance of power — the present balancing process — firmly but unknowingly supported by the Afro-Asian world, has been identified with international anarchy. Yet have we really attempted to comprehensively understand a process in which all of us have been participating? Have we attempted to estimate the forces that support this process and to perceive its more civilizing possibilities? In our part of the world we certainly have not; we have been busy condemning the Great Powers

[1] The balance of power, or the balancing process, may be worked "'destructively" if, as in the past, a state wishes to eliminate this process and substitute for it a process worked by a hegemonial system. But it may also be worked "destructively" if the true nature of the process is not fully understood or if there is an irrational antipathy against having anything to do with it. This was the cardinal error of United States policy after World War I. We are more fortunate because India, in fact, is following a normative balance policy; but we hardly know it or admit it, thinking we are keeping our hands "clean." Such thinking could lead to grave consequences to our country and to the world. [Author's note.]

for following balance of power policies, and in preaching sermons to them whilst denying that we preach sermons to anyone! Sooner or later we shall have to accept the responsibilities of a Great Power status in Asia. It is best that we begin to look around us with a more knowing eye, and realize that we live in a strange international environment, uncertainly poised between ultimate savagery and growing civilization; that the nuclear equilibrium was an unavoidable dilemma, and that, revolted as we are, and as all decent people are in any part of the world, by the total destruction it threatens humanity, it has nevertheless the potentialities of encouraging civilized growth to an extent never before made possible in any other historical phase of the balance of power.

Having arrived at a definition of the balance of power, and having explained it, we are in a better position to examine the nature of our foreign policy. Too much emphasis was placed by Indian writers, thinkers and publicists in the 1950s on the ideological basis of India's non-alignment. Whereas there is an undoubted measure of truth in seeing a country's foreign policy as a reflection of its domestic cultural traditions and ways of thinking and feeling, yet, in foreign affairs, these have, at the most, an incidental influence. Even today this is not appreciated, and most of our publicists, as well as our scholars, continue to emphasise the role of Indian cultural traditions in our foreign policy. No doubt our temperament is more peace-loving than of some of our close neighbours: our philosophical and religious thought bears evidence of this, although we should not forget that we have also produced a political thinker like Kautilya. Yet Mr. Nehru's first instinct in 1947, or earlier, must have been to look to the emerging world situation, before shaping the foreign policy of his country. It was the feasibility, the practicality, of the policy, which in all probability, must have been Mr. Nehru's first consideration. This needs to be said lest non-alignment develop into a creed in this country, as it is threatening to do, instead of remaining a rational policy which we might have to discard some day should the world situation change.

Moreover, these large ideological claims do us disservice in the eyes of the intelligent common man abroad, who has come to believe that such talk is mere eye-wash, that Indians are facile dissemblers, hiding a basic opportunism under the mask of ancient cultural heritage, which it is absurd to pretend can have great relevance to her external relations in the modern world.

To a great degree, whatever Nehru may have said or believed, non-alignment is effective as a policy because of the latent threat of alignment which it unmistakeably holds out.[2] This is a great deal similar to the policy England had pursued *with regard to Continental Europe* for the greater part of the 19th century. The so-called British "isolation" from continental affairs carried at all times a masked threat of intervention, and later, even of alignment. The British needed a fragmentation of power on the European continent so as to be free to pursue their interests overseas and keep them secure. Now and again they would interfere to see that the continental fragmentation of power was not unduly disturbed, and then withdraw. But at no time in the last century did they show a marked willingness to enter into a permanent pact or alliance. Even the so-called policy of equilibration was not as religiously fol-

lowed as the policy of fragmentation of power. . . . I say this because India's non-alignment is not, in any fundamental sense, different from Britain's European policy in the 19th century. We, too, are actively engaged in working the balancing process by refusing to be linked permanently to any other power or to grouping of existing alliances; yet our non-involvement, . . . carries a latent possibility, if not an actual threat of alignment. Through this we oppose the power of both sides; we confront their power with ours, and thereby help to lessen or to divide their potential might *vis-a-vis* each other and the world. Then again, the aim of our foreign policy is to maintain our sovereign independence intact and to continue to be a sovereign power *within* a society of other sovereign powers. (Hence our almost feverish insistence that all states should subscribe to the principles of *Panchsheel* or the five principles of peaceful co-existence). This, then, is a fairly good example of a "normative" balance of power policy manipulated by a large power. Indeed, non-alignment is no new manifestation; it is but a particular balance of power policy to suit the particular circumstances of India's position in the world, even as American and Russian policies are from their respective points of view.

But it is the realities of nuclear technology that have made possible and effective our particular balance of power policy. Non-alignment owes its effectiveness to the difficulty the two Super Powers are experiencing in resolving their conflicts by an ultimate resort to war. It is the "unthinkability" of an all-out war that has persuaded these Great Powers to act with great caution and circumspection in achieving the objectives, through means other than war. If Nehru, in 1947, had felt that war between the two world antagonists was very likely, he would have found it impossible to effectively operate his foreign policy, if he had at all been bold enough to adopt it. For the one striking difference between United Kingdom's position throughout the 19th century and India's after 1947, is that

[2] Of course one can hardly expect Indian foreign policy statements, however candid, to admit this. Usually we have emphasized that we wish to steer clear of all power blocs. We have maintained that the essence of non-alignment lies in keeping away from power blocs as much as possible. There is always the danger, of course, of some of our men in the Foreign Ministry becoming falsely theoretical about non-alignment (and cling to it when it may need to be discarded) because they fail to understand its intrinsic nature. Nor are many of our intellectuals immune to this error. Most policy statements about non-alignment are taken at their face value by those whose first business is to critically analyse them: to distinguish between political statements and the hidden, but much more real, implications underlying them. By and large they have refused to see that the threat of alignment, direct or indirect, underlies a non-aligned stance in foreign affairs. We refuse to consider the various possibilities which may make us aligned some day. [Author's note.]

the former had enough military power to pose a potent threat to other states: her geographical position and her naval supremacy enabled her to get away with non-involvement. India, on the other hand, was a starveling in 1947. Yet nuclear technology made all the difference to this starveling: it gave India almost all the power she needed to manoeuvre effectively in foreign relations and to pose something like a "threat" to both the alliance structures. . . .

War having become unthinkable non-alignment has become possible. In this sense non-alignment has historical uniqueness. It is a product of the Cold War and particularly of the nuclear "balance of terror."[3] But it is to represent non-alignment falsely if it is projected as a policy of abstention from power-politics or as a refusal to follow the old bad ways of the balance of power. This would be utterly incorrect. It is not merely the aligned world which indulges in a balance of power policy: Indian non-alignment is in every facet such a policy — although it seeks to be a normative one. What is baffling about our conduct of international affairs is not what we practice but what we preach. And Mr. Nehru must be credited and blamed, respectively, for both our good fortune and our self-deception.

This may, perhaps, become clear if we examine the much-emphasised relation between non-alignment and peace. We have placed great emphasis on "the pursuit of peace." Nehru repeatedly maintained that peace to us was a necessity and an ideal. No one can deny the sincerity of these utterances. Yet, every time in our brief history, when there was a clash between the "pursuit of peace" and defence against any form of territorial aggrandisement, we did not hesitate to take up arms to defend our territories. At such critical moments, our political leaders told us that we value peace, but not at the expense of our territorial integrity.

Naturally so. But if this is "naturally

so," we cannot maintain that the primary objective of our policy is peace; the primary objective, quite obviously and quite sensibly, is the maintenance of our territorial and political integrity. That has a priority above all other objectives. Now this is characteristic of any balance policy; peace has never been the *primary* object of a balance of power policy; the true objective of a balance policy has been the preservation of the sovereignty of the state which practices it, and that of a normative balance policy, the active pursuit of maintaining one's sovereignty *within* a society of independent sovereign states. We value peace more, no doubt, than some of our neighbours. But this does not justify the claim we often make that peace is above all our objective; the military clashes with China and Pakistan revealed these objectives to be different. No doubt we may not have been the first to provoke, the first to invade: we fought in self-defence. Nevertheless, we took to arms for an objective we regarded as being infinitely more precious than peace. And in the Goa incident we did not even make that pretence. . . .

However, the much-emphasised relation between non-alignment and peace cannot be so casually dismissed. Aren't we supposed to be a bridge between the East and the West? Have not our attitudes fostered more objectivity, and have they not served to impart a greater degree of responsibility to the statements of the leaders of both parties to the Cold War? Have we not created a sort of "cordon sanitaire" in international affairs, thus helping somewhat to clear the atmosphere in which these affairs are conducted? Have we not fostered a "temper of peace" in international relations by emphasising that negotiation is the only intelligent method of settling disputes in the nuclear age? In brief hasn't non-alignment contributed greatly to the climate of peace in international affairs?

None of these claims can be altogether denied; what has not been particularly stressed, even by our scholars, is that many of these objectives are meant to support an international "status quo," particularly fa-

[3] The mistake that has been often made by us is to identify the balance of power with this nuclear "balance of terror." . . . [Author's note.]

vourable to India. A conflict between the two Super-Powers has every possibility of escalating into a nuclear war. This would be almost as disastrous for India as it would be for the two Great Powers. Any major war between the great Powers is likely to affect the present international *status quo,* making the fate of a large country like India uncertain, if not altogether perilous. Therefore, a war between the great Powers, nuclear or conventional, is not particularly to our advantage. But wars waged against a country like South Africa or against Southern Rhodesia or against the Portuguese possessions in Africa or India, or a colonial conflict waged in order to expel a colonial Power from its colonial dependency — such wars have our firm support. For, apart from helping us to be in the swim with African and Asian countries, such wars are necessary to bring about a *status quo* even more favourable to India than that which prevails in these areas today. . . .

It is not, then, the maintenance of peace that is our primary concern but the maintenance of our international position as a sovereign nation within a society of sovereign nations. The significance of this policy — the policy of a potentially great Asian Power — lies not so much on its peace-strengthening capacities as in its sincere desire to continue to live as a sovereign state within a society of independent sovereign nations. A large power, such as India, pursuing such policies, should be aware that it must needs use its influence in a particular cause, should the need arise; that it should be ready and willing to shoulder even the burden of war in pursuit of these larger aims: for it is a rare phenomenon in international affairs when the good of one's country becomes intimately associated with the larger good of the world. Non-alignment, since 1947, has served these purposes well enough; events have vindicated our contention that by being non-aligned we have been able to serve ourselves and the world. But it is not inconceivable that a policy of *alignment* may, in the future, become necessary to

serve the same ends: *it is these ends we need to keep remembering.* For non-alignment, more essentially understood, is a national policy aimed at the perpetuation of the international society of sovereign states, in the circumstances of the post-war world — and, within this society, the maintenance of the sovereign independence of the states which practice it. Underlying it is a belief, that due to certain geographical and other factors, alignment would not serve the *same ends* as effectively. Nehru must have had something of this in mind when, before an American audience, he declared: "Where freedom is menaced or justice threatened, or where aggression takes place, we cannot and shall not be neutral. . . . The great democracy of the United States of America will, I feel sure, understand and appreciate our approach to life's problems because it could not have any other aim or a different ideal. Friendship and co-operation between our two countries are, therefore, natural. I stand here to offer both in the pursuit of justice, liberty and peace."

This then, is the essential link between the world's great democracies and ourselves, however much we may clash with them. It has been maintained that the United States has been interested in us because we are a democracy. Yet the true American interest does not lie in the "correspondence" of our internal forms of government: it lies in the essential correspondence in our aims in foreign affairs. No doubt the United States is interested in our experiment in democracy: but that is so because a change in the form of government in this country could very conceivably lead to a change in our foreign policy, gravely affecting the security of the United States. To use the terminology of this paper, the United States interest in us lies in the realization that a democratically organized India is likely to continue to follow a truly normative balance of power foreign policy, and not adopt a balance policy which, at best, is indifferent to the larger considerations characteristic of such normative policies.

Which, of course, does not mean that we cannot come in conflict with the United States. Two normative balance of power policies may clash with each other, though fundamentally they may be in agreement. The British and the Russians were bitter enemies throughout the 19th century over the Eastern Question; yet they came together in World War I against Germany. So may, in the future, the United States and the U.S.S.R., against Communist China. Our resistance to the United States is based squarely on one important rule of the balance of power. To resist and divide the strength of any power which threatens to have the means, even if it does not have the intention, of achieving hegemony. In the circumstances of the nuclear age, even a Power which did not have any intention of being hegemonial, may be induced to adopt such policies. Without Russia's resistance to the United States, for example, the now-free colonial world would have appeared to the United States a dangerous vacuum, which, if they did not fill, others might, ultimately posing a potent threat to United States security. . . . This is always the incipient danger, to the participating states, of the operation of the balancing process; a giant, as Nehru maintained, cannot help behaving like a giant sometimes. It is such considerations that underlie Asian and African resistance to American military pacts: the fear that the United States might become too dominant in the region and be tempted to pass from a normative balance of power policy to a hegemonial one. Non-alignment, which to a large extent depends upon the existence of these pacts, nevertheless feels it must shout at them and denounce them. Fundamentally akin though American and Indian interests may be, it is naive to believe that they will not clash at other levels, as long as the balancing process is operated by both. This is the dilemma and the challenge of international politics: geography and technology create the dilemma and pose the challenge to all that is worthwhile in human ingenuity. . . .

Evolution and Permanence

ARTHUR LALL

The writer of the final selection served as India's Permanent Representative and Ambassador to the United Nations from 1955 to 1959. He is now Adjunct Professor of International Affairs at Columbia University. Lall begins his review of persistent and changing elements in Indian foreign policy with mention of his belief in the ability of Indian culture to assimilate and synthesize various ideas and institutions, leading to an "intuitive" approach to external affairs. Sometimes called the "Indian mind" view of Indian society and politics, Lall's first premise has been shared by India's former President, Sarvepalli Radhakrishnan, a distinguished philosopher, and Chester Bowles, twice United States Ambassador to India. Other Indian and Western observers of Indian affairs do not subscribe to this premise which makes possible resolutions of apparent contradictions in Indian thought and practice. After introducing India's external orientation as a product of India's long history and complex civilization, Lall surveys the major events in the state's foreign relations and suggests how and why Indian nonalignment may have developed since independence. Certain ideals and interests continue, however. The Lall framework is meant to encompass several criticisms and defenses. Whatever final judgment is made about the strengths and weaknesses of Indian nonalignment, the diplomatic record and emerging issues interpreted here will have to be a major part of the subject matter under evaluation.

Prime Minister Jawaharlal Nehru died in May 1964. Not long before he died India was involved in a sharp clash with a major power, China, and suffered a quick military reverse. During Lal Bahadur Shastri's relatively brief tenure as Prime Minister India was engaged in another military conflict. This time [in hostilities with Pakistan in September, 1965] India was not defeated, but aspects of the fighting brought out the inadequacy of her largely antiquated defensive posture compared with the attack capabilities of more modern military equipment. These practical factors and the accumulation by India of general experience in international affairs have encouraged the belief that Delhi's outlook on world affairs has been changing recently, and might well be entering a new phase.

This view must be carefully assayed in the light of the main factors that influence and mold India's approaches to international affairs. In view of the length and the largely unrevolutionized character of the Indian tradition, probably the best point of departure in this endeavor is what might be described as the intuitive factor. This is the factor that gives expression to inchoate tendencies and spontaneous attitudes springing from deeply ingrained elements in the Indian scene. Obviously, it is beyond the scope of this brief study to delve into this point for a full exploration. Nevertheless, it is necessary to remind ourselves that in dealing with India we are con-

From Arthur Lall, "Change and Continuity in India's Foreign Policy," *Orbis*, X (Spring 1966), 91–105, selections. Reprinted by permission.

102

cerned with a society that has endured over the course of several millennia and developed, in this long process, a strong tendency to synthesize and assimilate rather than to espouse or reject.

It would be an oversimplification to say that India never makes an about turn in its attitudes, but it would be safe to say that hitherto Indian history and its movements have not developed along such lines. Therefore, at any given moment of time in India the conditioning of a very long past is a powerful factor in the formulation of policy, more powerful perhaps than in most other countries. Note, for example, the fact that in his first official broadcast to the Indian peoples, on September 7, 1946 — a few days after he had taken office as Vice President of the Executive Council of the Viceroy of India and almost a year prior to the attainment of independence by India — Nehru, who at that time had had no official experience in foreign affairs, not even in a parliamentary opposition party, stated in remarkably full outline the foreign policy which he was to implement for the next seventeen and one-half years. It was all there: nonalignment but an active foreign policy of full participation in world affairs, anti-colonialism and opposition to racist policies, international cooperation to create one world, the continuance of good relations with the Commonwealth always saving India's opposition to the policies of South Africa (at that time a member of the Commonwealth), acknowledgment of the great international responsibilities placed on the United States and the Soviet Union, and India's special relations with the vast Asian world. In this last category fell India's relations with the U.S.S.R. and China. Regarding the former, he said: "They are our neighbours in Asia and inevitably we shall have to undertake many common tasks and have much to do with each other." China (not yet taken over by the communists) he described as "our neighbour which has been our friend through the ages and that friendship will endure and grow."

How was it that, although he had had no official experience in foreign affairs or government, Nehru could outline a policy which has continued to shape India's external posture for the last twenty years? Of course, he was a keen student of world affairs, and his training had been cosmopolitan, but these personal factors do not explain the sureness of touch that we see in his first pronouncement on foreign policy. Deeper still was another impelling factor that persuasively directed Nehru's thinking. This was India's long practice over the millennia of the arts of synthesis and assimilation. It is in the stream of that long practice that there is room for India's friendship both with an anticommunist West and a communist Russia, for remaining within the Commonwealth while opposing the colonial policies of London in the years when the United Kingdom was still an important colonial power (and now, too, in regard to British policies in and around Aden and in certain parts of Africa), and for constant support for disarmament and other steps to reduce tension or neutralize trouble spots.

It is of primary importance to understand that this way of thinking that lay at the root of Nehru's first broadcast remains strongly operative in India. The severest test of India's non-alignment came when the Chinese forces penetrated into the country in 1962. The test was all the more severe because Nehru was somewhat behind rather than in front of the march of events, and, therefore, when the clash came the shock to him was all the greater. He could not believe that relations with China could or would deteriorate as they did in the late 1950's and the early 1960's. As late as December 1958, some time after it had become known in Delhi that the Chinese had established a number of posts in the Aksai Chin area of Ladakh, Nehru, true to the intuitive approach to foreign affairs which derives from India's long history, said in the Indian Parliament: "The normal idea is that security is protected by armies. That is only partly true; it is equally true that security is protected by policies. A deliberate policy of friendship with other countries goes farther in gaining security than almost anything else." . . . When Chou En-lai was in Delhi in 1960 Nehru said at the banquet in honor of the Chinese Prime Minister: "We have opposed not only war but what is called the cold war because this represented the approach of hatred and violence. We have endeavoured to follow, in our limited and imperfect way, the teachings of two great sons of India, the Buddha and Gandhi." The implication was that India was very far from thinking in terms of war.

The immediate effect of the Chinese-Indian war of 1962, however, was to call into question the basic pillars of India's foreign policy. Criticism was strong in the country and in Parliament. Nehru himself said that India had been living in an unreal world, and that "we are growing too soft and taking things for granted." But he clung tenaciously to the old lines of policy: "We are not going to give up our basic principles because of our present difficulty."

His successors have not only reaffirmed their resolve to cling to old lines of policy, but have moved in a measure — albeit still tentatively — toward negotiation until there was acceptance by China of all the provisions of the proposals offered as a basis of negotiation by the six Colombo Powers. Recently there have been indications that India would be willing to consider negotiations if there were some intimation by Peking of a readiness to negotiate. As long ago as December 1964 Prime Minister Shastri said that India was prepared for talks with China consistent with her self-respect. He was saying, in other words, that if the intention of China was really to arrive at a settlement and if Peking would not put forward at the negotiating table claims to large areas of territory with threats to take them by force, then there could be negotiations between the two countries. A year later, Shastri, referring specifically to India's relations with China (as well as those with Pakistan), said a day would come when the countries of Asia would have to sit down together and reach accord on a path to peace.

Under the new regime of Mrs. Indira Gandhi, talk of negotiation with China has increased. Jayaprakash Narayan, whose name means much in India although he is not now active in politics, said at a public meeting on February 2, 1966, that the Colombo proposals were now "dead." He called for fresh efforts to solve Sino-Indian disputes and suggested that the head of a state such as the U.A.R., Rumania or Tanzania should play a role toward this end. On February 16, 1966, speaking in Parliament after the Defense Minister of India had made a statement on border incursions by the Chinese, Mrs. Gandhi said that India was prepared to talk with China "should proper conditions arise." The very vagueness of this phrase places it in the category of a diplomatic feeler; although there is not yet any indication from Peking of a response, it is not unlikely that in the near future we will see that steps toward negotiation are being taken by both sides. In any event, these tentative moves by India may be regarded as some evidence of a return toward what one might call the normalcy of Indian foreign policy, the policy which Nehru said went back to roots some 2,500 years old.

There are some in India who are impatient with the tradition and would like to see some radical shifts in Indian policy. But even in regard to China, where the reasons for such a shift are prima facie very strong, I believe it has not in fact occurred. Should there be further significant military ventures on the border and should China rebuff the tentative indications of readiness to negotiate, we might still come to see some real changes in Indian policies, but it is wholly premature to predict such a development. In this connection it is relevant that India's President [Radhakrishnan], though his constitutional position is closely analogous to that of a constitutional monarch, exercises his considerable influence in favor of the search for a way to honorable negotiations with China.

For its part, perhaps, Communist China

might be inhibited from responding to the current Indian overtures because she has apparently convinced herself that India is joing a "U.S.-dominated anti-China front." On the other hand Chinese leaders are probably aware that Prime Minister Gandhi, speaking in Parliament on March 1, 1966, rejected suggestions that India should enter pacts for containing the Chinese in Southeast Asia. Mrs. Gandhi was of the view that such pacts were not conducive to peace, and might in fact increase tension and impinge on India's independence of policy. It cannot be ruled out that China might see negotiations with India as a strategy of averting or neutralizing any adoption by India of a posture opposed to Chinese interests. It must be remembered that even membership by Pakistan in SEATO and CENTO has not prevented the development of close relations between that country and China. These considerations are brought into focus not to develop a prognostication, one way or the other, regarding future Chinese moves, but because they are germane to a fuller understanding of Indian policy toward China at this time. If, in spite of the continuing aftermath of the border dispute — mainly in the form of exchanges of sharp diplomatic notes and other expressions of mutual suspicion — responsible voices can be raised in India in favor of negotiations with China, then we must admit the strength of the intuitive and traditional attitudes that influence the formulation of India's approaches to foreign policy.

Nehru's seminal broadcast of September 1946 did not touch on Indo-Pakistani relations for the simple reason that Pakistan did not come into being until almost a year later. Despite his reluctance to accept the division of the old India — this solution was by no means his first choice for the subcontinent's problems — his basic approach was to regard Pakistan as a fraternal state with which India must develop familial relations. . . .

There is no question but that the division of the subcontinent has created fundamental problems of power imbalance in Asia and has established a situation in which outside powers are able to exploit the division in their own interests. This preliminary statement is necessary for an appreciation of the complexities which confront Indian foreign policy in much of Asia.

At the Bandung Conference in 1955, Chou En-lai, although at the time apparently friendly with Indian leaders, could not but notice sharp exchanges between them and the Pakistani leaders. Consequently, he took Prime Minister Mohammad Ali aside and said to him that although Pakistan was a member of SEATO, China still regarded it as a friend. This was encouraging news for Pakistan, but for India it meant that in the Asian hinterland she was confronted with the possibility of a wide arc of hostility. In these circumstances, no Indian government could take seriously the view that the solution of the Kashmir issue would bring about permanent good relations with Pakistan if such a solution were based on the ceding of any more territory in North India to its neighbor. Supposing India agreed to an arrangement which gave the Kashmir valley or a substantial part of it to Pakistan, the strategic implication would be that China and Pakistan could join forces easily over the head of India. . . .

What, then, are the practical options open to India in respect of policies toward Pakistan? . . . One conceivable option is to make some small territorial adjustments of such a character that both sides could save face. If the recent war has had a really sobering effect on both countries a mutual accommodation on these lines — rather than a solution, a word that generally carries overtones of a tidy settlement — is conceivable. It should not stand alone. With it should go other developments to improve relations between the two countries, without in any way diminishing the separate sovereignties of India and Pakistan.

It would be naive and wholly impracticable to suggest any undoing of the partition of the subcontinent. But it would be almost equally naive to read into the future of the subcontinent and the surrounding areas an era of peace unless both India and and Pakistan recognize frankly that, while remaining separate entities and states, they must both accept a primacy of relationship *inter se.* If either continues to put before its relations with the other its relations with a third or more countries there will be the constant prospect of the intrusion into the subcontinent of outside adventurism to the detriment of the peace of the area. . . .

It is sometimes said that India has moved toward greater friendliness with the Soviet Union as her confrontation with China has developed. I do not think this view corresponds with the facts. In his policy broadcast of 1946, Nehru suggested that India and the Soviet Union would inevitably have to undertake many common tasks and would have much to do with each other. This has remained a constant pivot of Indian policy. In one's vicinage one must have meaningful friendships: this is true for all states. India and the Soviet Union, in spite of the differences between their political and economic systems, have sought and developed mutually friendly relations. Differences with other neighbors may have, from time to time, highlighted their friendship, but it is not true that those differences have caused the two to come together: that *rapprochement* has been determined by broad common interests in the peace of the area and of the world, by the requirements of India's economic plans, and also by India's desire to render such assistance as it could to improve relations between the West and the U.S.S.R. This last endeavor could not have been implemented at all if India had been cold or hostile toward the Soviet Union.

In the "pristinity" of Nehru's policy there is no reason why India should not be as friendly with the U.S.S.R. as with the Western world, and particularly with the United States. This of course does not mean that in all matters India should try to equate the actions and policies of the two superpowers. It does mean, however, that in each situation, be it Vienam or the

Dominican Republic on the one hand, or Hungary on the other, India should bring to bear an equal degree of understanding. India's reticence in 1956 with regard to the Soviet Union's action in Hungary was widely criticized, but not generally known were the very considerable efforts being made by India at the United Nations, Moscow, Budapest and elsewhere to counsel restraint on all those concerned. Not an exact parallel, but in some ways analogous, is the striking fact that in his statement in the general debate at the Twentieth Session of the UN General Assembly, on October 12, 1965, Sardar Swaran Singh, India's Foreign Minister, was unique among the representatives of the more important countries in not mentioning the Vietnamese situation. Since it is a well established tradition that the general debate statements of foreign ministers or other senior representatives of governments made at the General Assembly constitute overall statements of foreign policy, the omission was, of course, deliberate and was explained solely by India's desire not to cause embarrassment to those directly involved in Vietnam. India's reticence over issues such as Hungary or India's support for the Soviet Union in certain matters (e.g., some aspects of the Soviet plan for general and complete disarmament) are remarked upon in the Western press and in some sections of the Indian press and thus become obtrusive. On the other hand, the reticence of India in regard to issues that trouble her Western friends often goes unnoticed and is thus consigned to public oblivion. . . .

Recently, encouraged in part by indications that Pakistan's relations with the West are not as staunch as they have been, Moscow has shown more receptiveness to Pakistani overtures. This development is not detrimental to India's interests. On the contrary, it made it possible for Premier Kosygin to invite President Ayub Khan and Prime Minister Shastri to Tashkent last January to what turned out to be a significant conference on Indo-Pakistani relations. The U.S.S.R.'s widening interest in the affairs of the subcontinent has been welcomed by India. . . .

In some of the foregoing remarks we have touched on India's outlook toward the United States. . . . Central to this Indian attitude is the acknowledgement that the United States has vast and onerous world responsibilities. If at times there have been differences of opinion as to how these responsibilities might best be expressed and discharged, particularly in relation to India, its neighbors and other states of Asia, this is no negation of the general recognition by India of Washington's responsibilities. In this connection it is relevant that India, as the initiator and major formulator of the post-World War II policy of nonalignment at a time when alignment against Soviet communism was an essential credential for acceptance in certain Western circles, faced a difficult task in the conduct of its relations with the United States through most of the 1950's. However, since the commencement of the Kennedy Administration there has been a much greater degree of acceptance of nonalignment — which is by now the official posture in world affairs of some sixty countries.

Other elements in India's attitude toward the United States include recognition that, although great hazards accompany the possession of great power, the United States has yielded its power in such a manner that the world has avoided major conflicts. India is also unqualifiedly grateful for the large measure of economic assistance provided by the United States, especially in times of crisis such as the present food shortage. . . .

On the matter of assistance generally, India will carefully observe U.S. policy in regard to arms deliveries to Pakistan, which ceased during the short Indo-Pakistani war last year, as did deliveries to India. Perhaps here is an opportunity which should be seized by India and Pakistan to limit their respective defense establishments, under the control arrangements mentioned earlier. Then, if supplies were made to the two countries within mutually agreed limits,

suspicion on the subcontinent would be considerably allayed and criticism of U.S. policies in this field would diminish.[1]

On the question of Vietnam the same Presidential address to the opening of the budget session of the Indian Parliament on February 14, 1966, stated: "We are deeply concerned about the present situation in Vietnam. Any effort to resolve this conflict by peaceful methods will receive our support." Following Vice President Humphrey's [February 1966] visit to India, Prime Minister Indira Gandhi gave a more precise description of the Indian position when, in response to a question in Parliament, she confirmed that the Vice President had asked for India's support for the U.S. solution of the Vietnam problem. According to reports, Mrs. Gandhi replied that she explained to the American Vice President India's commitment to a policy of nonalignment and its "special responsibilities as chairman of the International Control Commission."[2] It seems clear that India will not abandon her policy of nonalignment even in her quest for good relations with the great powers. At the same time it is only fair to remember that India's leaders are convinced that nonalignment does not inhibit, much less preclude, the development of good relations with the United States and other states.

At no time has India claimed leadership of the nonaligned world. But it is a plain matter of record that through the 1950's and the early 1960's her leaders did, in fact, enjoy by common consent a position of some pre-eminence among their nonaligned colleagues. This was in a measure a reflection of the personal stature of the late Jawaharlal Nehru, who nevertheless was always anxious to make it clear that he regarded

[1] To the displeasure of India, in April 1967 the United States declared that it would not resume arms deliveries to India or Pakistan. [Editor's note.]

[2] Based on the 1954 Geneva Agreement on Indochina, India is chairman of the International Commission for Supervision and Control for Vietnam on whcih Canada and Poland also serve. [Editor's note.]

others, particularly Tito and Nasser, as in
every respect equally important. During
Nehru's lifetime two developments occurred which inevitably affected India's
position. The first of these was the very
success of nonalignment as an international
posture. Nearly all African states professed
to adopt it, and enshrined it as an integral
part of the Charter of the Organization of
African Unity. Because of their understanding of nonalignment, many of these
African states were of the view that they
could not take sides against China when
her forces attacked India in 1962. The
spread of nonalignment has made a degree
of polycentrism inevitable.

The second factor which adversely
affected India's stature in the nonaligned
world was the rapid success of the Chinese
in their armed attack against India in 1962.
Power is respected in the international
community. It had been assumed that big
India was reasonably strong. China was,
of course, assumed to be powerful, and it
was thought that in a military confrontation
between the two there would be a meeting
of two Asian giants. It turned out to be
quite otherwise, and this could not but
affect India's prestige. But the result of
that episode was not just the humiliation
of India. It split Asia and caused wide
repercussions. . . .

Though there have been these and other
loosenings of the texture of nonalignment,
it cannot be precluded that India will return to a position of some consequence
internationally. She has certain obvious
advantages and assets, and the buffets of
international events have convinced her
that she must build a strong economy and
strengthen her armed forces, while at the
same time she rediscovers the moral
strength that has been part of the Gandhian heritage, which is also a manifestation of her long tradition. It was in keeping with that heritage that Lal Bahadur
Shastri worked so hard for the Tashkent
agreement; and the recent tentative feelers
toward negotiation with Peking are also in
keeping with that heritage.

What India seems to lack now, in com-
parison with the greater part of the Nehru
period when she was in the forefront of
those states that contributed proposals for
the bridging of differences between the
main protagonists, is the capacity to demonstrate leadership in the world community.
This is to be explained partly by the fact
that India's leaders are preoccupied now
with the deployment of national capacities
for dealing with basic economic tasks such
as food production, communications and
transport. Added to this is the feeling that
in her state of exposed general power de-
bility she must first build her own overall
strength.

How far will the design for a strengthened India go? Will India build the atomic
bomb? Speaking in the Indian Parliament
on March 1, 1966, Mrs. Gandhi again rejected the suggestion that India should
manufacture the bomb. On the other hand,
India and other nonaligned countries have
repeatedly stated in the past year or two
that, if there is to be a meaningful nonproliferation agreement, the present nuclear powers must simultaneously agree to
take steps to achieve a degree of nuclear
disarmament and to make the nuclear test
band treaty comprehensive and universal.
What if these conditions remain unful-
filled — a most likely eventuality? In this
connection, Indians are apprehensive about
several facts, including Pakistan's nonad-
herence (a position shared only by Guinea,
Rumania, Mali, Cuba and France) to the
resolution [on November 23, 1965] at the
Twentieth Session of the General Assembly on the nonproliferation of nuclear
weapons. Indian leaders feel strongly that
they should have pressed harder for disarmament agreements which might have precluded the development of the Chinese
bomb; now they are concerned that if India
sits back while Pakistan, Indonesia and
others develop such weapons it would be
more than any Indian government could
justify to its peoples. This indicates the
seriousness and urgency of making world-
wide arrangements to arrest the spread of

nuclear weapons, which requires, *inter alia,* bringing China into the councils of the world community and instituting more purposeful talks on disarmament and arms control than those now in train at Geneva in the absence of France and China.

The pressures which India strives to create for a nonproliferation agreement to be accompanied by a degree of nuclear disarmament and a comprehensive and universal test ban treaty do not include the use of threats that she might break loose from her self-imposed restraint (India and Japan are the only countries in Asia that are known to be exercising genuine restraints in this regard) on the development of nuclear weapons. India fears, however, that if the great powers do not accept some form of nuclear disarmament there will almost certainly be untoward consequences.

India herself is psychologically unprepared for the manufacture of nuclear weapons. The old foreign policy of India basically remains intact, and though subjected to various distorting forces it shows a strong tendency to continue in the channels foreseen for it by Nehru in 1946. It is most unlikely that India will be the next country to enter the nuclear club, but if and when there is another entrant she will feel obliged, though reluctant, to follow suit. . . .

SUGGESTIONS FOR ADDITIONAL READING

The study of Indian nonalignment leads to a sizable bibliography which can only be introduced here. These suggestions are made on the assumption that India's independent foreign policy must be seen through understandings of the origins, conditions, and problems of what collectively is called Indian foreign policy, but that is actually a group of policies of which nonalignment is a central one.

Surveys of Indian foreign relations since freedom are found in Richard L. Park's contribution to *Foreign Policies in World Politics*, ed. Roy C. Macridis, 3rd ed. (Englewood Cliffs, 1967), in W. Norman Brown, *The United States and India and Pakistan*, rev. ed. (Cambridge, Mass., 1963), and in the chapter by Angadipuran Appadorai in *Foreign Policies in a World of Change*, eds. Joseph E. Black and Kenneth W. Thompson (New York, 1963). More extensive accounts are K. P. Karunakaran, *India in World Affairs*, 2 vols. (Calcutta, 1952 and 1958), surveying 1947–53; and M. S. Rajan, *India in World Affairs* (New York, 1964), covering 1953–56. India's relations with the West from 1947–54 are examined in J. C. Kundra, *Indian Foreign Policy* (Gronigen, 1955). Economic development and foreign aid are stressed in Barbara Ward, *India and the West*, rev. ed. (New York, 1964). A study of the external policies and internal dynamics of India and Pakistan is Norman D. Palmer, *South Asia and United States Policy* (Boston, 1966).

Nehru's political thought as a source of Indian foreign policies may be examined in M. N. Das, *The Political Philosophy of Jawaharlal Nehru* (London, 1961); Michael Brecher, *Nehru: A Political Biography* (London, 1959); Frank Moraes, *Jawaharlal Nehru* (New York, 1956); and Donald E. Smith, *Nehru and Democracy* (Bombay, 1958). These volumes are useful for their bibliographies of Nehru's many writings. *India's Foreign Policy* (New Delhi, 1961) presents many of his views from 1946–61. Nehru's revised socialism and mature reflections appear in "The Basic Approach," an appendix of Vincent Sheean, *Nehru: The Years of Power* (New York, 1960). A posthumous study is Walter R. Crocker, *Nehru* (London, 1966). An interpretation of Nehru as Gandhi's student is Willard Range, *Jawaharlal Nehru's World View* (Athens, Georgia, 1961). Gandhi's implications for international relations are assessed in Paul F. Power, *Gandhi on World Affairs* (London, 1961). Nonalignment is associated with Gandhian ethics in K. S. Murty, *Indian Foreign Policy* (Calcutta, 1964).

The Machiavellian tradition in Indian political thought is indebted to *Kautilya's Arthaśāstra*, tr. by Rr. Shamasastry, 4th ed. (London, 1952). A study of this tradition is George Modelski, "Kautilya: Foreign Policy and International System in the Ancient Hindu World," *American Political Science Review*, 58 (September 1964). The tradition of *dharma* or righteousness is interpreted in K. P. Mukerji, *The State* (Madras, 1952). British India's place in international relations is examined in Taraknath Das, *India in World Politics* (New York, 1924) and Bisheshwar Prasad, *Foundations of India's Foreign Policy* (Calcutta, 1955). A study of the Congress party and world affairs up to freedom is Bimla Prasad, *The Origins of Indian Foreign Policy*, 2nd ed. (Calcutta, 1962). Antiimperialism is explored in Richard M. Fontera, "Anti-Colonialism as a Basic Indian Foreign Policy," *Western Political Quarterly*, 13 (June 1960).

Indian policy and attitudes toward Kashmir and Pakistan are studied in Sisir Gupta, *Kashmir* (New Delhi, 1966), and his book *India's Relations with Pakistan* (New Delhi, 1958), treating the years 1954 to 1957. The Pakistani outlook may be found in M. M. R. Khan, *The United Nations and Kashmir* (Djakarta, 1955). See also Ayub Khan, "Pakistan's Approach to World Problems," *United Asia,* 14 (November, 1962). Experienced observers offer their accounts in Lord Birdwood, *India and Pakistan: A Continent Decides* (New York, 1954); and Joseph Korbel, *Danger in Kashmir* (Princeton, 1954). Several Indian writers interpret the background and events of the 1965 Indo-Pakistani conflict in *International Studies,* 8 (July, 1966).

According to many Indians, India's membership in the Commonwealth is not inconsistent with nonalignment because India secured its terms of association. The background is surveyed in Percival Spear, *India, Pakistan, and the West,* 2nd ed. (London, 1952). More specialized are M. S. Rajan, *The Post-War Transformation of the Commonwealth* (Bombay, 1963); and *India and the Commonwealth,* 2 vols. (New Delhi, 1954), edited, respectively, by K. P. Karunakaran and B. N. Ganguli. Membership in the United Nations brought a different set of opportunities and problems. India's conduct in the United Nations may be studied with the help of Ross N. Berkes and Mohinder S. Bedi, *The Diplomacy of India* (Stanford, 1958), which finds some flaws in applying ideals. More conventional is *India and the United Nations* (New York, 1957), an Indian Council of World Affairs study.

Within Asia India's policies are interpreted in Werner Levi, *Free India in Asia* (Minneapolis, 1952); and Norman D. Palmer, "India's Position in Asia," *Journal of International Affairs,* 17 (No. 2, 1963). The Institute of Pacific Relations has published V. P. Dutt, *India's Foreign Policy with Special Reference to Asia and the Pacific* (New York, 1950); and V. P. Dutt and Vishal Singh, *Indian Policy and Attitudes Towards Indo-China and SEATO* (New York, 1954). The Indian Council of World Affairs sponsored *Defense and Security in the Indian Ocean Area* (Bombay, 1958). The diplomat-historian K. M. Panikkar is

concerned with this topic in his writings especially *India and the Indian Ocean* (London, 1962.) Quincy Wright interprets India's action against Portuguese India in "Goa Incident," *American Journal of International Law,* 56 (July, 1962). Indian and Western opinion about the Goa episode is reviewed in Louis Dupree, "India's Move Into Goa," *American Universities Field Staff Reports Service: South Asia Series,* 6 (February, 1962).

The Sino-Indian dispute has produced a considerable literature. From the Indian side, see P. C. Chakravarti, *India-China Relations* (Bloomington, 1961); Girilal Jain, *Panchsheela and After* (Bombay, 1960); and V. P. Dutt, *China's Foreign Policy* (Bombay, 1964). K. M. Panikkar interprets his diplomatic role and Nehru's China policy in a memoir, *In Two Chinas* (London, 1955). Nehru's thoughts after the 1962 border crisis may be found in his "Changing India," *Foreign Affairs,* 41 (April, 1963). Documentary sources include *Report of the Officials of the Government of India and the People's Republic of China on the Boundary Question* (New Delhi, 1961); and the numerous *White Papers* of the Indian government, beginning in 1959. China's views may be located in *Documents on the Sino-Indian Boundary Question* (Peking, 1960); *Selected Documents on Sino-Indian Relations* (Peking, 1962); and *Peking Review.* About the struggle between the two Asian states these sources offer insight: Margaret W. Fisher and Joan V. Bondurant, *Indian Views of Sino-Indian Relations* (Bergeley, 1956); Margaret W. Fisher, Leo E. Rose and Robert A. Huttenback, *Himalayan Battleground* (New York, 1963); P. P. Karan, "The India-China Boundary Dispute," *Journal of Geography,* 58 (January, 1960); and Klaus H. Pringsheim, "China, India and Their Himalayan Border," *Asian Survey,* III (October, 1963).

The crisis in Indian foreign policy with the collapse of its China policy in late 1962 raised questions about nonalignment and the record of Nehru's stewardship. Although they have criticisms, contributors vindicate nonalignment in the Indian monthly *Seminar*, No. 45 (May, 1963). Unlike most Indians, Patwant Singh, in *India and the Future of Asia* (New York, 1966) argues for alignment with the West. A defense is N. R. Deshpande, "National Interest and India's Policy of Non-Alignment," *Indian Journal of Political Science*, 25 (January-March, 1964). Views critical of the Nehru bequest are found in A. B. Shah, ed., *India's Defense and Foreign Policies* (Bombay, 1966). Paul F. Power, "Indian Foreign Policy: The Age of Nehru," *The Review of Politics*, 26 (April, 1964) focuses on the Indian leader. Analysis of Indian reappraisals of foreign policy is offered by Werner Levi, "Indian Neutralism Reconsidered," *Pacific Affairs*, 37 (Summer, 1964); P. J. Eldridge, "India's Nonalignment Policy Reviewed," *Australian Outlook*, 19 (August, 1965); and Balgit Singh, "Pundits and Panchsheela," *Background*, 9 (No. 2, 1966).

Indian nonalignment and Russian-Indian relations may be studied with the aid of the following. K. P. S. Menon, *The Flying Troika* (London, 1963), is by India's ambassador to Moscow, 1952–61. K. M. Panikkar is the author of "Middle Ground Between America and Russia: An Indian View," *Foreign Affairs*, 32 (January, 1954). The often unstable history of Indian Communism is depicted in John H. Kautsky, *Moscow and the Communist Party of India* (Cambridge and New York, 1956), and Gene D. Overstreet and Marshall Windmiller, *Communism in India* (Berkeley and Los Angeles, 1959). An important background book is Chattar Singh Samra, *India and Anglo-Soviet Relations: 1917–1947* (Bombay, 1959). An article pointing out India's post-1962 dependency on Russia is Selig S. Harrison, "Troubled India and Her Neighbors," *Foreign Affairs*, 43 (January, 1965).

The writing on relations between the United States and India is a developed field. An early study is L. K. Rosinger,

India and the United States (New York, 1950). A product of the Council on Foreign Relations and the Indian Council of World Afiairs is Phillips Talbot and S. L. Poplai, *India and America* (New York, 1958). *India and the United States*, ed. Selig S. Harrison (New York, 1961) reports on a 1961 conference in Washington of specialists from both nations. Well-known is Chester Bowles, *Ambassador's Report* (New York, 1954). Papers sympathetic to India are Vincent Sheean, "The Case for India," *Foreign Affairs*, 30 (October, 1951), and E. Malcom Hause, "India: Noncommitted and Nonaligned," *Western Political Quarterly*, 13 (March, 1960). Shared democratic principles are stressed in Richard L. Park, "Bases for Political Accord Between India and America," *The Indian Yearbook of International Affairs: 1957*. Economic relations are studied in Charles Wolff, Jr., *Foreign Aid: Theory and Practice in Southern Asia* (Princeton, 1960). American images of India are examined in Harold Issacs, *Scratches on Our Minds* (New York, 1958). Jawaharlal Nehru, *Visit to America* (New York, 1958); and V. L. Pandit, "India's Foreign Policy," *Foreign Affairs*, 34 (April, 1965) reveal official Indian views of the United States. *India News*, published by the Indian Embassy in Washington, carries material of interest to the American public.

The study of nonalignment in world politics may help to clarify India's policy. Critical essays are in *Neutralism and Nonalignment*, ed. Lawrence W. Martin (New York, 1962). Less critical papers are found in "Nonalignment in Foreign Affairs," *The Annals*, 362 (November, 1965). *Outside the Contest*, ed. K. P. Karunakaran (New Delhi, 1963) is essentially sympathetic to nonalignment. Comparative studies are G. H. Jansen, *Afro-Asia and Nonalignment* (New York, 1966); and Peter Lyon, *Neutralism* (Leicester, 1963). Attempts to analyze the elusive concept are found in N. P. Nayar, "Growth of Nonalignment in World Affairs," *India Quarterly*, 18 (January-March, 1962); and F. Low-Beer, "The Concept of Neutralism," *American Political Science Review*, 58 (June, 1964).

Bibliographic aids include a critical review of English language books dealing with Indian foreign policy in Bimla Prasad, "Survey of Recent Research," *International Studies*, 5 (April, 1964). Indispensable are the annual bibliographical issues of *International Studies* and *The Journal of Asian Studies*. Bibliographies with pertinent listings are Patrick Wilson, *Government and Politics in India and Pakistan: 1855–1955* (Berkeley, 1956); M. L. P. Patterson and R. B. Inden, *South Asia: An Introductory Bibliography* (Chicago, 1962); and J. Michael Mahar, *India: A Critical Bibliography* (Tucson, 1964). For current developments the *Asian Recorder*, the *Foreign Affairs Record* and the *Indian Press Digests* are useful.